Patches Of Sunshine

(A Daily Devotional For Fibromyalgia Patients)

Nancy Sonneman

AmErica House
Baltimore

First printing

ISBN: 1-58851-729-2
PUBLISHED BY AMERICA HOUSE BOOK PUBLISHERS
www.publishamerica.com
Baltimore

Printed in the United States of America

DEDICATION

To Sheila my Spiritual mentor,

to Bruce and "Cholly" who taught me how to use the computer and are my "techno-support",

to Patti who encouraged me to write in the first place,

to Rose who gave me my first "break" in her newsletter,

to my Mom who has been more than patient through this whole process,

and especially to God who called me to write this book, gave me the words, and the ability to write them down.

INTRODUCTION

This book was written *for* Christian Fibromyalgia patients, *by* a Christian Fibromyalgia patient.

For those uninitiated, Fibromyalgia is incurable. It is not terminal, it is something we die with, not from. One description of this syndrome is that it is a cross between arthritis and the on-set of the old-fashioned flu.

Symptoms of this syndrome are as follows: mental fatigue (also known in Fibromyalgia lingo as "brain fog"), migraine headaches, memory problems, sound hypersensitivity, loss of some sound frequencies in hearing, light sensitivity, blurred vision, decreased peripheral vision, TMJ pain (in the jaw), taste sensitivity, allergies, shoulder bursitis, heart palpitations, mitral valve prolapse, shortness of breath, numbness and tingling in hands and feet as well as cold hands and feet, hypoglycemia, acid reflux, irritable bowel and/or bladder syndrome, incontinence and/or enuresis, morning stiffness, overall physical fatigue, chronic fatigue syndrome, tendonitis, and hypersensitivity to being touched.

The symptoms can come in any combination.

As anyone who has ever battled (or seen someone battle) chronic illness knows, it is not easy. If a disease or injury comes along, family and friends need only be sympathetic for a little while before the patient returns to normal. When it effects the rest of a patient's life, it also effects family and friends (who may or may not be willing to go along for the ride). After a while, relationships become strained as the "normal" family and friends struggle to cope right along with (or maybe even more so) than the patient himself or herself. This book is designed to help with the "coping" part.

*

HOW TO USE THIS BOOK

The first step in dealing with a syndrome as unpredictable as Fibromyalgia is to:

1) Find a positive role model. I can't think of anyone more positive than He is.

2) Keep a positive attitude. That is what this book is about. Staying positive, no matter what.

3) Remember, although we have Fibromyalgia, it does not have us. Try to keep our lives as normal as we possibly can with no whining and

complaining.

4) Use this book like any other devotional, but know that it was written by someone who has been there, and wants to help others get so caught up in seeking God's face that there is no time for the pain.

JANUARY

January 1st

Listen to this, all you people! Pay attention, everyone in the world!

PSALM 49:1

Can you imagine Jesus, hands cupped around His mouth, calling to the chosen twelve? How about God using his big, big megaphone to yell to us over the din of our modern world? Are we even listening anymore? For those of us Fibromyalgia patients, hearing the Word is even more vital, so is giving our days to Him. It is my goal to gets us-and keep us-focusing on Heaven (and away from the symptoms), and keeping it light and easy. Life is too short not to listen to God. Can you imagine not wanting to hear Him?

Dear God; Thank you for a brand new year. Let my attitude keep it sparkling new for each of the remaining 364 days. Help me to pay attention to you always. Amen.

*

January 2nd

Listen to my prayer, O God. Do not ignore my cry for help.

PSALM 55:1

When I was a kid, we had a dog. He was a poodle and weighed all of five pounds full grown. His hearing was excellent, from a can of dog food being pulled out of a grocery bag to the mail truck brakes squeaking two blocks away. I knew he wasn't deaf, and I came to realize that he wasn't ignoring me when I gave him a command he didn't want to deal with just then (I could see his ears twitching). Maybe the same is true with God? He isn't deaf and he isn't ignoring us. Even though we can't see His ears twitch, we know He is listening. Maybe He knows we couldn't deal with it just then. Anyway, I kept calling to our little dog until he answered, and I am going to do the same with God.

Dear God; Fibromyalgia affords me the luxury of relying on You more. Thank you, Jesus. Never let me forget to say "Thank You". Amen and Amen.

January 3rd
You quieted the raging oceans with their pounding waves and silenced the shouting of the nations.

PSALM 65:7

The last time I was in the ocean, I could not get out! The waves had pounded on the shore enough to create a little lip so that the surf allowed my feet to clear it. At first, I thought it was funny. What I must have looked like, falling and struggling with the tumbling seashells! After swallowing enough salt water to keep several sharks alive, I was no longer laughing. A calmness came over me then. I knew He was telling me it would be all right. Once I stopped struggling and trying to solve the problem myself and put my trust where it belonged, I could finally walk right out of the ocean.

Dear God; Those of us who suffer migraines as part of Fibromyalgia can relate to the imagery in this verse!! How much it hurts and how good it feels when it stops! Let me never forget that it will stop. In Jesus' name. Amen.

*

January 4th
I am suffering and in pain. Rescue me, O God, by Your saving power.

PSALM 69:29

Why is it easier to pray when we are in pain? I never had much time to pray any other time. Yes, I had heard the sentence, "if you're too busy for God, you're too busy". I just never paid any attention to it. Then I bought a big, thick prayer book (I felt compelled to buy it. Like my hands wouldn't work even if I tried to put it back on the shelf) without much looking at its contents. This book and I belonged together. When I got it home and paged through it, I realized that about seventy-five percent of the book was for me, the intentions that I needed and still need. But I was still too busy. Then I heard a preacher on television say that Satan is always at work, and he loves to keep people from communicating with God, and the less you communicate with God, the easier it is to backslide and/or fall completely away. Now, my prayer time is first thing every morning and last thing every night. E-mail, and any other interruptions can wait. It's a struggle, sometimes, to keep my focus on the prayers and off my planner, but it is worth it. I want to put God first in my life, so I start the day with Him. God is never too busy for me, so I'm no longer too busy for God.

Dear God; Although Fibromyalgia is the bane of my existence, it won't be the focus of it. Since I have it, help me to fold it up and put it in my back pocket so I can take it with me as I go about leading my life. In Jesus' name. Amen.

*

January 5th
For as a man thinketh in his heart, so is he.... (AMP)
PROVERBS 23:7

While rummaging around in a box in the basement, I found the hairbrush I used to use as a "microphone" while I pretended to be the latest pop sensation when I was a kid. Imagination was my favorite "toy". I could go anywhere and do anything I wanted. Now, I realize that my thought life really does have a lot to do with my real life. IF I think and talk negatives, my life will be negative. I have seen examples of people who do nothing but complain and crab, living miserable lives, not to mention making others miserable along the way. Keeping a positive attitude is fun, just like the box that became a rocket ship or racecar (depending on my thoughts), and even though I never really could sing (with or without my hairbrush), my world that God gave me is just as beautiful as I can imagine.

Dear God; If I tell myself I'm "up" and enthusiastic, I will be. What a wonderful thing attitude can be. Help me keep my mind focused on You and my attitude pointed in the right direction and all will be well. Amen.

*

January 6th
I will lie down in peace and sleep, for You alone, O Lord, will keep me safe.
PSALM 4:8

Have you ever noticed that The Ten Commandments don't come with a disclaimer that says "no longer applies when tired"? The more tired I get, the less I pretend to care that I'm not acting like Jesus. In short I act like a toddler in need of a nap, (which I sometimes treat myself to). I spend the day just about to boil over. My late grandmother used to tease that if were a teapot, I'd whistle! I tell myself that if it wouldn't bother me any other time, why is it on my nerves now?

Dear God; The chronic fatigue portion of Fibromyalgia gets old after awhile. Fill me with more peace than usual on days after sleepless nights and bless me with sleep for the next night. Amen.

*

January 7th

Finishing is better than starting. Patience is better than pride.

ECCLESIASTES 7:8

A few years ago, without consulting the Lord, I decided that I would treat myself to a guitar and lessons. Mind you, my singing sounds like a foghorn at worst and a bullfrog at best. I can't even stand the sound of my own voice. After my fifth lesson, and being no better of a guitarist than the day I walked into the music store, I bought a metronome. While practicing that night, I realized that I played straight through the metronome without as much as even feeling "the beat" of the metronome. I put it in my guitar case, then put an ad in the local newspaper to sell the guitar. I sold it two days later for much less than I paid for it. Not everyone is good at everything. Some have talent for one thing, some for another. I now seek God before any such decisions, and I have learned the most important thing to finish is whatever God tells me to.

Dear God; You are the only one who knows how many times I was gung-ho to start a project only to have it lie around half-or one-fourth-started. I confess this sin and promise not only to finish what I start, but also to include You in the decision-making process so that together we choose only what I can handle.

*

January 8th

Be strong and very courageous. Obey all the laws Moses gave you. Do not turn away from them and you will be successful in all you do.

JOSHUA 1:7

Last Sunday, a cricket decided to join us for worship. At first, I thought it might be a Charismatic with as much noise as it was making. Then I thought it was auditioning for our choir as it seemed to "sing" along. As the service progressed, our little visitor got louder and louder. It was starting to be annoying. I was really struggling to keep my attention where it belonged. The cricket kept going until church was dismissed. It was all I could do to keep my eyes riveted on the pulpit instead of letting them roam the room to attempt to locate the annoyance. Had I given in, I would have gotten as much out of it as if I had stayed home. Whenever I have been tempted, I think of that cricket. That sound is now my signal to pour on the strength!

Dear God; Obeying Your laws does take strength and courage. Please help me to have that as I attempt to live the way You want me to.

*

January 9th

The sovereign Lord is my strength! He will make me as surefooted as a deer and bring me safely over the mountains.

HABAKKUK 3:19

"Surefoot" was my nickname when I was a kid because I was anything but. I made klutzes look like gymnasts. One time, we went to an outdoor performance of our Pops Orchestra. It was held in a park, so everyone brought blankets and picnics. My aunt and I were on our way back to our blanket from the restroom. Trying not to step on the other blankets took some doing because it was crowded and looked like one big crazy quilt. With my next step, I tripped over my own feet and fell in the middle of one family's take-out chicken dinner! Fortunately, they were finished eating (and very understanding). My laughter covered my embarrassment, but it was their laughter that saved the day.

Dear God; The imagery that I get here is enormous! In Heaven, there will be no pain, no weakness, no Fibromyalgia; only breath-taking beauty and the chance to catch up on every ability that I do not have here. Until then, You give me strength to hope in You. Amen.

*

January 10th

You must love the Lord your God with all your heart, all your soul, and all your mind.

MATTHEW 22:37

My mind wanders. Complete with "Gone Fishing" sign. The worst is that it wanders during Bible study and prayer time. This isn't "brain fog", it is a hazard of the profession because most of the time I'm thinking about a project, but it is really a lack of discipline. I just can't seem to bring my mind to the obedience of Jesus. I love Him with every fiber of my being, but you sure couldn't tell it if you read my mind. I make sure I work at this every day, though, because I want to be a whole Christian!

Dear God; Help me follow this commandment so well that it becomes like breathing. Thank You. Amen.

*

January 11th

Don't copy the behavior and customs of this world, but let God transform you into a new person by changing the way you think. Then you will know what God wants you to do, and you will know how good and pleasing and perfect His will really is.

ROMANS 12:2

A few years ago, the company I worked for wanted to bring in uniforms. It was voted down because most people didn't want to dress alike. But when we went to "casual Friday" mostly everyone wore jeans and t-shirts, looking like everyone else. Behaviors that once were considered shocking and/or shameful are now accepted without so much as a batted eye. Subjects that were once taboo are now seen in the number one television shows and movies. No one seems to know what "wrong" is because the mentality seems to be "everyone is doing it" (no matter what "it" is). I'd rather keep my focus on the Potter to see what He can do with this lump of clay.

Dear God; Conformity is the theme of this world. I am delighted that You are constantly changing me to be the person You want me to be. Amen.

*

January 12th

...Act on the principles of love and justice, and always live in confident dependence on your God.

HOSEA 12:6

To teach myself to listen and obey the Father, I try to give Him even the smallest decisions. When I was younger, I used to make a list of what to wear for a week, no matter how the weather here in the Mid-West changes. Now, I ask God what He wants me to wear the next day, and I'm lead right to it in the morning. The best part is, I never have to iron or replace buttons at the last minute, either.

Dear God; Help me to take what You give me and share those gifts with everyone. Thank You. Amen.

*

January 13th
When I see the rainbow in the clouds, I will remember the eternal covenant between God and every living creature.

GENESIS 9:16

Rainbows have always been a favorite of mine. I loved to draw them when I was a child, and seeing them today as key chains, etc., still make me smile. One day we were out running errands just after a rainy morning. I came across a tiny puddle covering a spot of oil. With the little bit of sun hitting on it, there was a miniature rainbow. It took me back to the time when I was a kindergartner and saw a sight just like that. I was so excited.
"Look, Mommy, a rainbow! Just my size!" It would be many years before I realized the Biblical significance of rainbows. I just knew that they were special and having "one of my own" was even more special yet.

Dear God; Every time I see a rainbow, I realize how fortunate I am to have a God who has never or will never break a promise. I love You. You are so good. Amen.

*

January 14th
I love the Lord because He hears and answers my prayers.

PSALM 116:1

Sometimes it seems like God is on an extended coffee break. At times, I barely get the words out of my mouth before I get an answer. Other times, it seems like months that I pray for the same petition before I get an answer.

I know that God does things only for my good and in His own time. I'm the impatient one. I want everything, "now, now, now". I try to tell myself that God knows when things are best for me, that I couldn't handle things, maybe, before then. I know that God always hears me, I just have to wait for the answer. God always surprises me, it's fun!

Dear God; Help me to accept the answer "no" when it comes and to realize that everything You do is for my good. Amen.

*

January 15th

But when the Holy Spirit controls our lives, He will produce this kind of fruit in us: love, joy, peace, patience, kindness, goodness, faithfulness, gentleness, and self-control. Here there is no conflict with the law.

GALATIANS 5:22

Fruits aren't like gifts where just one or two are cultivated and polished. All of them need to be practiced on a daily basis. No excuses. We're to follow those fruits no matter how or what we're feeling. It isn't easy, but then it wasn't easy for Jesus to hang on the cross, either. Every day, I do what God expects of me - I try my very best.

Dear God; Whenever I think of this verse, I feel like a juggler. Trying to keep all the bowling pins in the air at the same times is quite a task. I can't seem to accomplish all of these fruits at once. But I'm not about to give up. I'm God's Child and that's just fine by me. Amen.

*

January 16th

Restore to me again the joy of Your salvation and make we willing to obey You.

PSALM 51:12

There was a time when I would have gone for the loophole angle. "Willing to obey" doesn't sat I actually have to obey, just be willing to obey. Now I realize that you don't follow The Ten Commandments by accident. Sometimes, something gets lost in the translation between "willing" and "obeying", but now I don't look for loopholes anymore. Nor do I make excuses. My Bible and teaching tapes are in use a lot now. I hope I never go back to looking for loopholes.

Dear God; Help me be willing to obey You every second of every minute of every day of every year for the rest of my life. Amen!

*

January 17th
Doing wrong is fun for a fool, while wise conduct is a pleasure for the wise.
PROVERBS 10:23

I still remember the exact day (the memory comes slower now, I have to recall it), but I won't record it here. Part of the grand-opening festivities here in my city included the appearance of a national television star. I could take or leave the show, but we went to the store nonetheless. Instead of the stage I thought he would appear on, he came down the aisle and shook hands with everyone. When he got to me, and I looked up at him, I saw a glimpse of Jesus. Instead of giving my life to Jesus, I got caught up in the celebrity's charisma. Before long, I was worshipping this celebrity to the point of substituting Jesus' name for this man's. This went on for eleven-and-a-half years. It wasn't until I made a retreat that God put on my heart that I was actually into idolatry with this man. I knew I had to turn to Jesus and give Him my life. I also knew that this man had to be purged from me in order for me to put my focus where it belongs. For the next six months, it was like withdrawal. I cried and rationalized and prayed. But God won out in the end. So much so that I can't recall life without Jesus being in charge.

Dear God; Help me in my constant struggle to use wise conduct. Thank You. Amen.

*

January 18th
A person's words can be life-giving water; words of true wisdom are as refreshing as a babbling brook.

PROVERBS 18:4

A woman that I worked with always seemed so sad. She had been injured in a long-ago car accident and missed many days of work due to its lingering effects. I knew her only to say "hello" to as we passed in the halls. I always wished there was something more I could do to help her in some way. Not long after she came to work with me, she became a grandmother for the very first time. The baby was a beautiful red-haired little girl. Whenever I would see this woman in the hall or at the copier, etc., I would ask, "How's your grandbaby?" Never have I seen such a transformation. The sadness fell away like a melting ice sculpture and she would smile a genuine smile of happiness, her eyes full of life as she prattled on about the baby. In this tiny way, I feel like I helped this woman, yet it only took a few seconds on my part.

Dear God; Let all my words flow like a beautiful cascade today; do not let them stagnate like an algae-laden pond or spray at random like one of those constantly whirring sprinklers. In Jesus' name. Amen.

*

January 19th
But to those called by God to salvation, both Jews and Gentiles, Christ is the mighty power of God and the wonderful wisdom of God.
1 CORINTHIANS 1:24

In today's world, the mighty name of Jesus is used as a curse word so often. I cringe every time I hear it. People seem to say it without as much as a second thought. Whenever people utter it as such, they should bite their tongues or have some other immediate small, yet painful malady befall them. This would continue until people got the idea; that's a no-no and should be substituted with something - anything - not a curse word, please, until this something becomes as habitual as taking the most exulted name in the universe in vain.

Dear God; It is impossible to understand or question Your power or Your wisdom. Christ is the mighty answer that You provided for Your people. All we have to do is realize and accept. Amen.

*

January 20th
They put the man in custody until the Lord's will in the matter became clear.
LEVITICUS 24:12

Sometimes I would like to put every decision " in custody" until the Lord shows me the right one. For instance, while I'm still in the parking lot for a day of shopping, I always quote Psalm 23:1, "The Lord is my shepherd, I shall not want." Hopefully, God will help me with control over my wallet. Whenever I stop to ask myself if I really need it, if it's appropriate to wear to that event, if it mirrors Christian Witness, etc., I know that it is actually God, giving His much sought after answer, and I obey.

Dear God; Help me to put my wallet, my fork and the rest of my own reasoning "in custody" until I can see Your will for me in any situation, no matter the significance I myself assign it. In Jesus' mighty name. Amen.

*

January 21st
If you are really eager to give, it isn't important how much you are able to give. God wants you to give what you have, not what you don't have.
2 CORINTHIANS 8:12

Our little poodle used to give of himself totally. I remember a fall down the steps I took and he came, tail wagging, concern in his eyes, a kiss as if to comfort me. When he was really glad to see us after a long, tough day, his whole body seemed to wag; turning circles, giving us a cute little look as if to say, "it's all right now. You can relax." No matter what I needed, he was always there, giving of himself tirelessly. There's a lesson to be learned here.

Dear God; Please help me to realize that giving doesn't always have to mean money. Giving of time and talent is giving of myself, which is better than money. Let me give selflessly today, with the right attitude, as much as I have to give. Amen.

*

January 22nd
For He is our God. We are the people He watches over, the sheep under His care. Oh, that you would listen to His voice today!
PSALM 95:7

I use television time to do other things (jigsaw puzzles, crafts, even reading during commercials) while I'm watching television. When someone comes into the room and asks the score or what the show is about, I haven't the first idea. It's as though I had drifted off to sleep. This used to be the way I prayed or read the Bible, while doing a multitude of other tasks. No wonder I never got an answer. If it had fallen on me, I would have missed it. Now I give my undivided attention to God and am amazed that I get His undivided attention back. I used to tell people that I believe in God, but He doesn't believe in me. How wrong I was! Once I learned that in order to be heard, I had to listen, I could not believe in the change in my walk with Him!

Dear God; Help me not whine or complain so I can hear Your voice. Amen.

*

January 23rd

Teach me how to live, O Lord. Lead me along the path of honesty, for my enemies are waiting for me to fall.

PSALM 27:11

During a retreat that I was participant of, one young woman complained that she wished there was an instruction book for life. Her best friend made up a book cover from a paper bag and wrote on it, "Life's Instruction Manual", and put the cover on the woman's Bible. Until then, I never thought of the Bible in that way. Since then, I have been reading the Bible through new eyes. Every book has verses that tell us how to live. I thought it was just The Ten Commandments in Exodus. Now I try to follow these instructions to the letter, and I discuss them with Him whenever I need advice.

Dear God; Let me listen to Your Word and then put it into practice. Amen.

*

January 24th

He renews my strength. He guides me along right paths, bringing honor to His name.

PSALM 23:3

One of the biggest changes in my life has been a tamping down of my temper over the years. This is so my Witness can glorify God. It used to be nothing for me to turn around and bite somebody's head off for the least little thing. As God began to deal with me, I began to try to sneak my temper bursts past God without Him noticing. As the snapping subsided little by little, I tried to get by with saying my snide little remarks under my breath. I could almost hear the Lord say, "I heard that!" I would outwardly cringe. Then I just thought my share and seethed in silence. Whenever I read the Bible, I was drawn to verses on peace. As I became blessed with peace, I began to realize that anger doesn't glorify God. Even though I still mess up on occasion, I am grateful to be able to have most of my behavior glorify God along the way.

Dear God; Alleluia! When my Fibromyalgia gets me down, You are always there to recharge my batteries so I may glorify Your name. Amen.

*

January 25th

Then an angel from heaven appeared and strengthened him.

LUKE 22:43

Jesus is always there to give "oomph" we need each day. He sends His angels to watch over and stand behind each and every one of us. Sometimes my angel puts his strong hands on my shoulders for comfort and protection, other times he stands behind me and literally gives me a shove into social situations to tell me, "you can do it, don't be shy." When I get lazy, my angel hands me the tools I need, points me in the right direction, and says only, "go", in a tone I know better than to argue with. Just before I fall asleep sometimes, I hear my angel whisper, "Sleep well. You've done a good job today." That's when I smile and snuggle down to peaceful sleep.

Dear God; Those of us who are in need of an extra little nudge are especially grateful for our angels. Thank You for helping us have a fighting chance to make it. In Jesus' name. Amen.

*

January 26th

Tell those who are rich in this world not to be proud and not to trust in their money, which will soon be gone. But their trust should be in the living God who richly gives us all we need for our enjoyment.

1 TIMOTHY 6:17

Enjoyment. When I got my first job, before I accepted my Savior, the trend was clothing with alligators on it. Those little alligators sent a message to the world that said, "I belong". I could barely wait to get my first credit card (you never bought trendy stuff with cash. Part of being trendy is flashing those credit cards around) so I could get my alligator apparel. When I got my beloved credit card, I bought so many things with alligators on them you would have thought I owned stock in the company. I really looked cool in my new clothes, and my snootier-than-thou attitude was all part of the "new me". Until the bill came. When saw it, I'm sure I looked like an alligator - a sickly shade of green. My Mom lent me the money that I had thirty days to pay back, and did the best thing she could have done - cut up my credit card. I've learned a lot about "enjoyment" since then and about how to enjoy what God has given me the right way.

Dear God; Thank You for helping me day-to-day, to get my focus off what the world says is important (food, clothes, career, etc.) and get it back on You where it belongs. In Jesus' name. Amen.

*

January 27th

He passed in front of Moses and said, "I am the Lord, I am the Lord, the merciful and gracious God. I am slow to anger and rich in unfailing love and faithfulness."

EXODUS 34:6

Isn't it great to know that we can mess up so royally and still be held in the biggest, softest, most loving arms we could ever imagine? God loves us so much and with such an indescribable, abundant love that it is simply beyond our understanding. We need to be reminded of that love as often as we can be. It serves as a real spirit-lifter and reminder of just who my life is for.

Dear God; You are so gracious and wonderful! We are blessed! Amen.

*

January 28th

Stop quarreling with God! If you agree with Him, you will have peace at last, and things will go well for you.

JOB 22:21

I'm getting better at this. I really am! Now that I know that the things God does are only for my good, I'm not as likely to fight. It isn't possible to win an argument with Him. He knows every thought before you can think it, so you can't get any leverage anyway. The more I know God and Jesus the more I know a loving father and best friend, so why would we ever want to quarrel with God in the first place?

Dear God; I come to You with hat in hand. I confess that I am stubborn and cranky sometimes and You are often a target of mine. Please help me to desire your peace more than the last word! Thank You. Amen.

*

January 29th
Don't be quick-tempered, for anger is the friend of fools.
ECCLESIASTES 7:9

Anger really does cloud up an otherwise beautiful day. What does it accomplish except to make everyone miserable? It keeps everything churned up and stirred up within me. Especially if I repeat the story throughout the day. "The more I talk about it, the madder I get"? Then don't talk about it. The whole world needs the same advice; take a deep breath, calm down, and stop letting Satan steal your joy.

Dear God; If I must be angry, help me dismiss it quickly and forget it ever happened, using Jesus' forgiveness of Peter's betrayal as my example. Then I can enjoy the rest of Your day. Amen.

*

January 30th
And I will give them singleness of heart and put a new spirit within them. I will take away their hearts of stone and give them tender hearts instead.
EZEKIEL 11:19

I knew a kid who ate, slept and breathed baseball. Her room was "wallpapered" with pictures of her favorite baseball players. Piled high beside her bed was every sports magazine on the market. Her parents and teachers wished she could have recited her school lessons the way she could rattle off statistics and game scores. This was in the days before sports channels and scrolling scores across the bottom of the screen. She did that for everyone willing to listen - and even those who weren't. Now that she is an adult with a family to take care of, baseball has long since taken a back seat. She is a born-again Christian and has been for many years. Now she can quote the Bible like she did with statistics and scores. Her heart belongs to Jesus now and eats, sleeps, and breathes Him now - like He wants all of us to. Like I strive to do, too.

Dear God; A tender heart is special, but only when we put it use is it's true value seen. Thank You. Amen.

*

January 31st
Let all who take refuge in You rejoice, let them sing joyful praises forever. Protect them so all who love Your name may be filled with joy.

PSALM 5:11

When I look around, the old adage of the glass half full or half empty rings true. It depends on how you look at His creation. Do I see a rainy days as "blah", as plans ruined or as necessary to revitalize the earth, as an opportunity to spend time together with family and/or friends? I love the calming sound of gentle rain on my window. It makes it so cozy! God gave us joy. It is up to us to find it.

Dear God; You have put the joy in my heart. I refuse to allow Satan to steal it. Jesus gave too much for me for that. Help me to keep the joy visible from the outside so that others want what I have. Amen.

FEBRUARY

February 1st
Wait patiently for the Lord. Be brave and courageous. Yes, wait patiently for the Lord.

PSALM 27:14

I have to remind myself to calmly read a book instead of glancing at my watch every few seconds, heaving audible sighs. This is true in grocery store lines and especially while I await an answer to a prayer or while I adjust to an answer that I've already been given that wasn't the one my flesh wanted.

Dear God; I keep reminding myself that it isn't that I wait, it's how I wait. That's the "courageous" part. If there is one thing Fibromyalgia has taught me, it is patience. For that lesson, I say "thank You". Amen.

*

February 2nd
Create in me a clean heart, O God. Renew a right spirit within me.

PSALM 51:10

Sometimes I feel like a naughty kid who got dirty after repeated requests to stay clean. It's pretty hard for that kid to hide the mud-caked shoes, the dirt splotched shirt, the jeans that once were blue under all the brown gook. That's what my soul probably looks like to God. Because I can't see it myself, it's easy to forget it's there (especially those little sins that show up as mud-spatters but still count like dumping the whole mud pie on me), or to deny myself that it exists - no matter the size of the stain. I used to wait to say my prayers until I was in bed at night, the only trouble was that I often fell asleep before getting even one quarter of the way finished. Now I have a realistic prayer schedule. Even so, I still have to remind myself of my dirty heart so one day I'll wear sparkling, brilliant white.

Dear God; I ask you to show me what I need to work on. Clean me top to toe, Lord, let me walk with You down the path You've chosen for me. When I stumble, please reach out and catch me so I don't fall completely. In Jesus' name. Amen.

February 3rd
The joyful shout and weeping mingled together in a loud commotion that could be heard far in the distance.

EZRA 3:13

Isn't it odd that it's more acceptable to rant and rave like a lunatic in public (at salesclerks, waitresses, etc.) than it is to have a bring-the-house-down display of pure joy? You're more likely to be led to a nice padded cell if you go around smiling all the time than you are if you go around scowling and crabbing all the time. The next time you're in a public place and can catch snippets of conversation, listen to how much negativity versus positivity there is. Shocking, isn't it? The joy of the Lord is bubbling up inside you. Don't bury it under society's negatives. We don't belong to this world, and I, for one, am glad.

Dear God; Jesus is Lord! I want to shout if from the rooftops! Let all the tears in my eyes today be tears of joy. In the name of my Savior. Amen.

*

February 4th
So I pray that God, who gives you hope, will keep you happy and full of peace as you believe in Him. May you overflow with hope through the power of the Holy Spirit.

ROMANS 15:13

The dictionary defines "hopeless" as "without hope, allowing no hope, causing despair." This word should not be allowed in the dictionary simply because it doesn't exist. As hard as it is to believe when we're going through tough times, there is no such thing as "hopeless". As long as we have faith, we have hope. No devil in hell can take it away from us. We need only remind ourselves of this when the storm comes, and we will indeed have "overflowing hope".

Dear God; "Overflow with hope", what a very generous wish for someone. Your power lies within me. Without hope, we are nothing. My happiness and peace will come from Your hope that always overflows in all of us! In Jesus' name. Amen.

February 5th

But you are not controlled by your sinful nature. You are controlled by the Spirit if you have the Spirit of God living in you. (and remember that those who do not have the Spirit of Christ living in them are not Christians at all.)

ROMANS 8:9

The other day, after promising God that I would cut out as much refined sugar from my diet as possible and cut all gluttony from my life, I went to one of those restaurants with a dessert bar. Only mere hours earlier, I had sincerely said a prayer for victory over gluttony. While I was dishing myself a huge helping of warm cherry cobbler, a slice of chocolate mousse pie, and a big white chocolate chip/macadamia nut cookie, I forgot my promise and my prayer. When I sat down at the table, I flashed onto that prayer and realized that I was in sin. Instead of pushing my plate away, I chose the taste of the food over the sweetness of the Lord. I've already repented for it, but I'll still be sorry when my clothes feel tight. My sinful nature doesn't usually win out, but I do have a free will that gets me in trouble from time to time.

Dear God; The Spirit is living in me. However, He is sleeping just now. I hereby awaken Him so we can squelch the sinful nature, squashing it like an unwanted bug. In Jesus' name. Amen.

*

February 6th

Deceit fills the hearts that are plotting evil; joy fills that hearts that are plotting peace.

PROVERBS 12:20

Have you ever noticed that there are no spaces in planners for peace? When someone plans a vacation, he or she wants "peace and quiet". Why just have it a couple of weeks out of the year? Jesus gifted us with peace to keep and utilize every minute of every day. Our world is so noisy (most of it which we take for granted; i.e. traffic, radio, etc.) that we really have to search for silence now. Why not start a trend and mark off fifteen minutes per day in your planner for peace (just to "be")?

Dear God; In order to plan peace, I have to draw on the gift of peace that Jesus gave me. Plotting evil is foreign to me, although the devil has tried to claim my heart. My heart belongs to Jesus, and I am planning peace! Amen.

February 7th

Why then does my suffering continue? Why is my wound so incurable? Your help seems as uncertain as a seasonal brook. It is like a spring that has gone dry.

JEREMIAN 15:18

I was the kid others made fun of. From Kindergarten through my Senior year in High School. When you're called "stupid" pretty much on a daily basis, you have a tendency to believe it. In no time at all, my self-respect was at sub-zero level. It's as fresh in my mind as if it had happened this morning. I was in third grade. One of the girls was having a birthday party that weekend so she methodically passed out invitations to everyone in class. Everyone but me. No physical pain I have ever endured before or since hurt like the pain of knowing that I was the only one excluded. No matter what you go through in life, He is always there as the light at the end of the tunnel.

Dear God; Praises! This type of thinking makes Satan happy. I will think only positive thoughts. In Jesus' name. Amen.

*

February 8th

And He said to her, "Daughter, your faith has made you well. Go in peace. You have been healed."

MARK 5:34

We handicap ourselves. I have known a lot of people that look perfectly fine on the outside but are basket cases on the inside. My concern now is to bring my thought life under His control. My body will be whole in Heaven, but my mind is going to determine whether I get there or not.

Dear God; Please heal my mind and emotions so that I am prepared for a healed body. Amen.

*

February 9th

May God bless you with His special favor and wonderful peace as you come to know Jesus, Our God and Lord, better and better.

2 PETER 1:2

Getting to know Jesus is fun. It is better than getting to know a best friend and solving the latest mystery three pages before the sleuth does all rolled into one. When I was a kid, I grew up in a church-going family. I knew about Jesus, but I didn't really know Him. Since accepting my Savior, I have been having a blast discovering my Very Best Friend. My favorite haunt is the local Christian bookstore. I'm learning not only to live for Him, but to live with Him as well.

Dear God; When we know Jesus, we know peace. Indescribable, unprecedented peace. In the name of our Messiah. Amen.

*

February 10th
Please be quiet! That's the smartest thing you could do.

JOB 13:5

There's an old adage that says, "it is better to keep your mouth closed and have people think you're a fool than it is to open your mouth and prove it." I've learned to quote this Bible verse to myself (on nearly an all-day basis sometimes) to keep myself out of trouble. There are times when I have to leave a situation to avoid spouting off. We're supposed to be "the intelligent animal". We couldn't prove it by our mouths sometimes.

Dear God; Help me realize that the ears are an even more important part of conversation than the mouth. By Your grace, let me have the wisdom to know when to use what. Amen.

*

February 11th
You love Him even though you have never seen Him. Though you do not see Him, you trust Him; and even now you are happy with a glorious, inexpressible joy.

1 PETER 1:8

The Bible does not give a physical description of Jesus. All we have to go on is artists' renditions, and that is sort of sketchy (pardon the pun) at best because all they had to go on was that fact that Jesus was a Jew (hence the dark hair and eyes). We only have what scientists tell us about the height of the average person in those days to estimate how tall He was. This makes the first day in Heaven seem that much more exciting. We'll finally get to see what He looks like!

Dear God; It's true, I have accepted You sight unseen. But You have seen and still You have accepted me. You are the reason I wear a smile so much. Thanks. Amen.

*

February 12th

And may the Lord give you wisdom and understanding, that you may obey the law of the Lord your God...

1 Chronicles 22:12

Wisdom and understanding seem to go hand-in-hand in the Bible. They seem virtually interchangeable. Maybe what we are supposed to understand is one another. It is easier to handle a rude clerk if you realize that he or she might be having a bad day or something weighing heavily on the heart or mind. We may be the only image of Him that person sees that day. A word or act of kindness may be all it takes to turn a day (or a life) around.

Dear God; Please help me to use the wisdom and understanding You gave me so I can take as many tomorrows as I have left and obey the Laws You gave Moses. Amen.

*

February 13th

Give thanks to Him who made the heavens so skillfully. His faithful love endures forever.

PSALM 136:5

Saying "thank you" is something I forget too often. Like any other parent, God loves to hear it. Like any other parent, He does not have to do any of the wonderful things He does for us. I'm learning to say "thank You" for the beauty of nature as I see it through the car window on the way to the grocery store, or for each body part I wash in the shower, or for a friend I've just spent time with, or just life itself. All too often we're so busy waiting for the major miracle that we forget the ones right under our noses.

Dear God; In the fickle society we live in, it's hard to imagine love being "forever". Help me be less fickle today, Jesus, and concentrate on Your example of "forever" with all that I do. In Jesus' name. Amen.

*

February 14th
Love never gives up, never loses faith, is always hopeful, and endures through every circumstance.

1 CORINTHIANS 13:7

Happy Valentine's Day, Jesus! Today is the day for lovers, and since Jesus is the best example of love there ever was (or ever will be) I don't want to exclude Him. I can't get Him a card or flowers or candy so I'll just have to try to follow His awesome example and reflect on His life and love.

Dear God; Help me to focus on and thank You for all that is right with me and forget about what is wrong. Amen.

*

February 15th
Good advice and success belong to Me. Insight and strength are Mine.

PROVERBS 8:14

"Success" is so highly stressed in today's world. Signs of "success" are the size of our homes, how many figures our paychecks have, and how many hi-tech toys we have. We see only the outer appearance, but God sees what's on the inside of us. Maybe success, like beauty, is in the eye of the beholder.

Dear God; Please help me to realize that the only way to turn is towards You in all matters. In Jesus' name. Amen.

*

February 16th
Study the Book of the Law continually. Meditate on it day and night so you may be sure to obey all that is written it.

JOSHUA 1:8

The only thing I want in my life is a close personal relationship with Him, to obey Him without hesitation (like breathing). Everybody nowadays has a tendency to overload his or her schedule (be it business or social or both), and then wonder why God never speaks to us. Do we ever speak to Him? Do we keep His Word in our hearts and minds? Do we apply it to our lives? I'm trying to be still and simplify, to get closer to Him. What a great feeling!

Dear God; Forgive me for not reading Your Word as often as I should. Help me to make time to hold Your Word always in my heart so I can put it into practice every day. Amen.

*

February 17th

...Get to know the God of your ancestors. Worship and serve Him with your whole heart and a willing mind. For the Lord sees every heart and understands and knows every plan and thought. If you seek Him, you will find Him. But if you forsake Him, He will forsake you.

1 CHRONICLES 28:9

Remember when you were a kid (or maybe you've said it to your own kids) and to keep you in line, your parents would tell you, "Santa Clause is watching you"? Well, God is always watching, listening and tuning in to us, no matter what. Keeping the correct thoughts in line with God's will twenty-four hours a day is a real challenge, to say the least. Like anything else, practice makes perfect.

Dear God; I don't know if I like the idea of Your knowing my thoughts sometimes, or not. Let me strive to honor You with every thought I think. Thank You. Amen.

*

February 18th

Then all of you can join together with one voice, giving praise and glory to God, the Father of our Lord Jesus Christ.

ROMANS 15:6

I love to hear music. Whether it's a solo performance or an entire chorus, I love to hear people sing as if with one voice. If there were more praise and worship leaders, there would be more choruses, which means more singing and less time to do much else. Like fume, fight, and war. This is what God had in mind. Praising Him so much that no one wants to do anything else.

Dear God; I lift my one voice in praise to You! Amen.

*

February 19th
Commit everything you do to the Lord. Trust Him, and He will help you.
PSALM 37:5

I make more Ishmaels than Israels in my life because I am impetuous. Rush right in first then think it over days later. I trust Him with every fiber of my being, yet I still make so much mess simply because I don't stop long enough to consult Him. Maybe I think I'll catch up to Him in mid-stream? Obviously, I am still working on this aspect of my Christian walk. In the meantime, I'm still praying about this.

Dear God; Forgive me for the times I rush headlong into things without consulting You (and then wonder why it turns into a huge mess). I do trust You with everything, no matter how tiny or how enormous. I just forget that from time to time. Help me to remember. Thank You. Amen.

*

February 20th
And endurance develops strength of character in us, and character strengthens our confident expectations of salvation.
ROMANS 5:4

Giving up is easy. I should know, I've done it often enough to know what I'm talking about. Endurance brings accomplishment and accomplishment feels so good. I want endurance to be part of my character. It takes inner strength - His strength - to keep going all the way to cross the finish line. But when the tape breaks across our chest and we realize we've made it - what a feeling, what a "high"! On the way, we can really enjoy the scenery.

Dear God; Endurance can often seem like climbing Mt. Everest. Help me remember the wonderful feeling ("view from the top") when all has been accomplished. If we are to run the race for the prize, we cannot quit or we will never receive our prize. Amen.

*

February 21st
I will tear down your walls and demolish the defenses of your cities.
MICAH 5:11

When I was a kid growing up, the term "defense-mechanism" was the pop-psychology catch phrase of the day. It excused anything and everything. Of course, everything was looked at a defense mechanism in the behavior pattern, whether it was or not. Clinging to God like moss on a rock wipes out our need for defense mechanisms and all of our walls. No matter what they are made of or how long they've been standing.

Dear God; I know You want us to cling to You only as our rock of refuge. Help me to see past all the "feel-goods" the world offers and run only to You for comfort. In Jesus' mighty name. Amen.

*

February 22nd
"In that day" says the Lord, "I will answer the pleading of the sky for clouds which will pour down water on the earth in answer to its cries for rain."
HOSEA 2:21

Ever since I was a kid, I've played "the cloud game". There is no better way to acknowledge God's presence that to watch the white wisps and puffs form images and shapes against an otherwise clear blue sky. It is awe-inspiring as well as freeing. As I spot angels, kittens, or elephants, I thank Him for the sheer delight I feel in His artwork. I also thank Him as I realize that the delight and joy last after this relaxing game.

Dear God; No matter what I need, Lord, You will meet it. For this I give You praise. Amen.

*

February 23rd
So humble yourselves before God. Resist the devil, and he will flee from you.
JAMES 4:7

The devil may flee when I rebuke, but he never seems to stay gone very long. The temptation (or whatever) seems to come racing back within seconds, even before I can get a full sentence of a prayer out. I always keep him on the run, though, as I rebuke and pray, rebuke and pray, rebuke and pray.

When God wins out as always, I remember to thank Him, sometimes again and again. With God on my side, Satan doesn't stand much of a chance.

Dear God; Some days all I seem to do is rebuke the enemy. Thank You for always providing us with an "out". Help me remember to take it and to stand strong. Amen.

*

February 24th
Your Word is a lamp for my feet and a light for my path.
PSALM 119:105

In those days, light came from only natural resources. In our day, we have all sorts of light; from flashlights to lighthouses (only a hand-clap away). It is sometimes hard to sort through all the man-made things to find "The Source". Picking up the Bible and opening it up to read is very illuminating. Virtually every verse can be used for our betterment. There's a catch, we have to use the Bible daily. The more we use it, the brighter our world becomes, until we are shining like the Son.

Dear God; Help me to get engrossed in Your Word today. The Bible; a book we shouldn't put down. Amen.

*

February 25th
Wisdom is a tree of life to those who embrace her; happy are those who hold her tightly.
PROVERBS 3:18

The tree in the backyard caddy-corner behind us, couldn't make up its mind if it did, indeed, want to be a tree or a just a tall bush. It was spindly, and craggy, and ugly, and I suspected more dead than alive. Yet it seemed to stand proudly, playing sentinel over the yard itself. One day, the city was hit with an ice storm. It looked like an illustration from a children's picture book. Everything was a glowing glaze. I walked into our family room to settle down with a cup of tea when the ugly little tree grabbed my attention. It was encased in ice and, with the sun hitting it, it looked like one those little spun glass crystal figurines. I gasped, shrieked, and ran for my camera. After I snapped a couple of pictures, I started to go back to a by-now room-temperature cup of tea when a strange thing happened; the little tree toppled over, unable to bear the extra weight. Then an even stranger thing happened, I began to cry like I had lost a member of my family. For years, the ugly little tree had been there. Taken for granted and not given much thought because of its appearance, it was like so many people I encounter on a daily basis. Yet because they are a creation of God, He often uses them for beauty in the most unexpected ways, if we could just realize this, the world would sparkle and shine just like that little tree.

Dear God; Trees are continually growing. Help my wisdom to grow and help me hang on for dear life. Amen.

*

February 26th
Jesus Christ is the same yesterday, today, and forever.

HEBREWS 13:8

I am not a parent, but I would think that the hardest part of being a parent would be consistency. My moods allow me to be a slob one day and a neat freak the next. Some days everything gets on my nerves, other times, nothing does. I try not to use "bad day" or "didn't sleep well" as excuses for ugly behavior. I also try to remember to thank God extra much for good, symptom-free days. I also thank Him that at least one of us is consistent in this crazy world.

Dear God; The same strong arms, the same gentleness, the same commandments, the same everything. Yet each new day brings new mercies, new possibilities for comfort, and for us to follow the perfect example. Thank You for Your stability. Amen.

February 27th
He is like the light of the morning, like the sunrise bursting forth in a cloudless sky, like the refreshing rains, that bring tender grass from the earth.

2 SAMUEL 23:4

My aunt looked forward from summer to summer because she always took her two-week vacation by traveling to various states via tours. She was single for a long time and saw many wonderful sites. The most beautiful of these, even close to thirty years later, she recalls was an early morning airplane ride. As the airplane began its decent, she glanced out of the window and did a "double-take". The sun was just coming out, just breaking through the clouds. Also breaking through the clouds was the peak of a mountain. With the sunny cloud around the peak, it looked as though the mountain was wearing a halo! My aunt said she had a sense of peace fill her that day that has lasted all these years. Even though this was away from home, He found her and blessed her with sunshine!

Dear God; If Your earth is so beautiful how much more so is Heaven? Let me reflect on this when the first prickles of depression strike. In Jesus' name. Amen.

*

February 28th
The Lord nurses them when they are sick and eases their pain and discomfort.

PSALM 41:3

The Bible doesn't promise that being a Christian means I'll never have a problem, but it promises that God will be there to guide me through no matter what. Sometimes, the fastest working "medicine" is comfort. Isn't it great to know that we have The Comforter whose existence it is to comfort, protect and guide us? We can go to Him anytime anywhere with anything. Maybe we aren't healed because God can use us better with problems than without. As for me, I'm just grateful that He's using me, period.

Dear God; Even if I'm not feeling so wonderful, help me realize that even though You haven't cured my Fibromyalgia, You're there to wipe my brow, give me my medication, and a much needed hug. Thank You. Amen.

MARCH

March 1st
But those who wait on the Lord will find new strength. They will fly high on wings like eagles. They will run and not grow weary. They will walk and not faint.

ISAIAH 40:31

"Free as a bird" is an old cliché. Maybe it's because from way up there, in the air, all our problems look so small, so the eagles believe that they are small. If we believe every problem is small and the only large thing is the image of Jesus on the cross, we can't help but wait on the Lord. Eagles make their home on the rock. That's where the freedom comes from.

Dear God; I'm looking forward to my "bird's eye view" of Your creation today. As always, I slip my tiny hand into Your enormous one with the knowledge that with You to guide me, I can run forever without weariness, and/or walk coast-to-coast without fainting. In Jesus' name. Amen.

*

March 2nd
"For I know the plans I have for you", says the Lord, "They are plans for good and not disaster."

PSALM 120:7

There are zillions of stories that begin with tragedy and end with triumph. As we go through it, well-meaning family and/or friends reminds us, "It's His will". Even though that's right on the nose, it isn't what we want to hear just then. Sometimes it takes years after the triumph for full realization or revelation to sink in. In the meantime, it's comforting to know that whatever life seems to throw at us, God always has a life preserver to throw, too, and it always makes a bigger splash.

Dear God: Whenever something happens that I don't understand, I remind myself of this verse, this truth. As I check my daily planner, I purposely leave room for You and Your will. Amen.

March 3rd
When he prays to God, he will be accepted. And God will restore him to good standing.

JOB 33:26

When something is too good to be true, it usually is. To protect ourselves, we become suspicious, even of things we should trust. Like God. Something so good, so wonderful, and so awesome. We can't believe that His unconditional love could be real, true, "just for me". No matter how great a love we have here on earth, it will never compare one drop to the love God has for us. Since we'll never understand it, I say we just enjoy it!

Dear God: Your agape is indescribable. It is beyond my understanding. No matter how bad anything in my life gets, the knowledge that your arms are always there to comfort me is the best medicine ever. Amen.

*

March 4th
You will have courage because you have hope. You will be protected and will rest in safety.

JOB 11:18

Learning to ride a two-wheeler was the biggest accomplishment of my little life. I had always watched "the big kids " soar into the street from their sloped driveways, watched them ride into the street, and I was enthralled. One day, I decided I had passed the threshold and was now a "big kid". We lived with my grandmother. All the driveways on that street looked like ski-slopes to a six-year-old. Not realizing that my mother was standing at the door, I mounted that pink-and - white bike so proudly. I got a running start back at the garage and I soared like a big, free bird. The only problem was, I was in such a hurry for adventure that I forgot to look both ways. The momentum carried me up into the across-the-street neighbor's driveway to safety. The car barreling down on me missed me by an eye-blink. I didn't even know what happened until my Grandma called me into the house. My Mom, ashen-faced and near tears, didn't know whether to hug me or slug me-but she chose the former. I then heard how I had nearly been killed. How good it felt to be safe!

Dear God; When I hurt, I wish I were a toddler again, so I could feel the protection of my Mother's lap which I have long since outgrown. I still have Your lap and the comfort of the knowledge that I will never outgrown it brings. Amen.

*

March 5th

Coral and valuable rock crystal are worthless in trying to get it. The price of wisdom is beyond pearls.

JOB 28:18

"Trying to get it". Every human being is born with a hole in the heart. Some attempt to cram the hole with an over-abundance of food, sex, drugs, alcohol, and material possessions. Some try career, the acquisition of money, and idolatry of "beautiful people". These only make the hole bigger and the cramming effort, spin even further out of control. The filler for the hole is God. He fits the hole just perfectly, patching it over until smooth. No other "possession " even comes close!

Dear God; How the world has come to idolize material possessions over Your gifts is beyond me. Please let my eyes never stray from You and Your prize. Amen.

*

March 6th

You will keep in perfect peace all who trust in You, whose thoughts are fixed on You.

ISAIAH 26:3

Here in America, our currency carries the slogan, "In God We Trust". It isn't just a slogan for most, it's a lifestyle. The world's message is "take charge of your life" and/or "you're in control". Because we hear so many scams and so much crime, we have become unwilling to trust. God earns our trust all the time, yet we aren't ready to give it to Him, at least not completely. It can be difficult, but how worth it in the long run.

Dear God; Keep my thoughts fixed on You so I may always enjoy Your peace. Amen.

March 7th

And the Father who knows all hearts knows what the Spirit is saying, for the Spirit pleads for us believers in harmony with God's own will.

ROMANS 8:27

"Procrastination" seems to be my middle name sometimes. One and a half years ago, I attended a nationally known preacher's three-day seminar. This preacher had an altar call for those who sought Baptism by the Holy Spirit. I was one of about one hundred. When the Holy Spirit was released upon me, I received one short syllable. Because I rarely use that now, I have never gotten any more (but because I have never gotten any more I rarely use it). Since it is His own language, and Satan doesn't understand it, what a marvelous gift, what a wonderful tool!

Dear God; Thank you, Holy Spirit, for your intercession. Amen.

*

March 8th

He always stands by His covenant- the commitment He made to a thousand generations.

1 CHRONICLES 16:15

My pet peeve is people who don't live up to their commitments. I've been to meetings that can't start on time because people are habitually late or classes where people habitually miss classes. I go by the fact that God has never broken a promise to me (which is a what a commitment is) nor will He ever break one, so I will never break a promise to Him.

Dear God; Let me live up to every commitment I have made and realize how important giving my word is. Amen.

*

March 9th

Be still in the presence of the Lord, and wait patiently for Him to act, Don't worry about evil people who prosper or fret about their wicked schemes.

PSALM 37:7

There was a story of the neighborhood's mean old woman. When I was growing up, she was called "The Witch", and it was said that her spooky old house was haunted. Hers was the biggest house on the block and I presume the story started due to flat out jealousy. Anyway, she kept a lot of animals in the yard, as well as an immaculate, expensive, never-driven car (she didn't even have a driver's license). She was rude and nasty to anyone who dared go into her yard or climb up her front steps. One day, years later, there was an ambulance in her driveway. The story came out that she was caring for her aged mother. She was an only child and had to give up her whole life, even the love of her life, for her mother. It was the inheritance that she got from her father that paid for the house. The car had been his (he had died suddenly) and the mother couldn't bear to part with it We never know what goes on within someone's home (or heart), but that doesn't stop us from passing judgment, does it ?

Dear God; Please remind me of what is and is not my business. Remind me also, that what is not my business should not still be in my mind. Help me to leave all things that are Your business to You alone. Amen.

*

March 10th
For when we place our faith in Christ Jesus, it makes no difference to God whether we are circumcised or not circumcised. What is important is faith expressing itself in love.

GALATIANS 5:6

Love is such a beautiful concept. Kindness. Just even a smile when someone is hurting can make all the difference. If we truly use Jesus as our example, we can't help but have a great love walk because Jesus is love. It doesn't have to be anything elaborate, a simple "thank you" to parent or spouse for even a tiny act shows love. Using good manners to strangers shows love. The ways are infinite.

Dear God; Every act of love someone is shown holds a mirror up to You and is actually an act of faith. Amen.

*

March 11th
I weep with grief, encourage me by Your Word.

PSALM 119:28

Right after my diagnosis, I began reading everything I could get my hands on about the syndrome. As more and more symptoms started falling in line, I became less and less positive. I thought my life was over. Then I volunteered to work at a local charity fund-raiser. A stream of about fifteen wheelchair-bound teenagers came in the door. It was then I realized how blessed I truly am. It also caused me to spend my break in repentance and Thanksgiving to the One who had seen fit to create me as I am. The "pity-party" habit was broken right then.

Dear God; I'm reminded that Fibromyalgia patients have physical limitations. Because of this, we have a tendency to grieve for ourselves. I pray that those of us experiencing self-grief don't succumb to a daylong (or lifelong) "pity party", but turn to Your Word and You for comfort and encouragement. In Jesus' might name. Amen.

*

March 12th
They grope in the darkness without a light. He makes them stagger like drunkards.

JOB 12;25

After a storm, complete with power outage, I decided it would be best to keep a flashlight beside my bed for just such occasions. Fortunately, such incidents are few and far between. When I needed my flashlight again, the batteries were no good At first, I was sort of panicky. Then I calmed down and told myself that Jesus was there with me so all would be well. It was then that my eyes adjusted to the dark and I noticed the moonlight coming in the window, to lead me safely out of the room. His light shines all the time. All we have to do is find and follow it.

Dear God; We stagger and stumble in the darkness, but we prevail and thrive in Your Light. Thank You for Your Light. Let our prayers be like paying our electric bill. In Jesus' name. Amen.

*

March 13th

As we talk to our God and Father about you, we think of your faithful work, your loving deed, and your continual anticipation of the return of our Lord Jesus Christ.

1 THESSALONIANS 1:3

On my desk first thing in the morning at work is often a fun little surprise. No one ever owns up to it, but I think I've got it narrowed down to a few suspects. I've always been one to say "thank you" and want to do something nice for the person.

The "fun little surprises" are probably purchased at the dollar store or the flea market, but they brighten my day and bring a smile to my face. Best of all, whoever is doing this is glorifying God.

Dear God; Help me to realize that any love I show for another today glorifies You, not me, or Jesus will not return for me. Amen.

*

March 14th

...And let us run with endurance the race that God has set before us.

HEBREWS 12:1

I enjoy watching "individual sports" (golf, tennis, diving, skiing, etc.). What fun to watch the smile of the winner who knows he or she used a God-given talent to his or her best ability. We all have been blessed with God-given talents to use to the best of our abilities, whether it be athletics, academics, etc. When I stand before His throne, I hope my own smile will be as bright.

Dear God; Help me run my lap of the race with integrity, love, faith, and trust in You. In Jesus' mighty name. Amen.

*

March 15th

Now He sits on the throne of the highest honor in heaven, at God's right hand. And the Father, as He had promised, gave Him the Holy Spirit to pour out upon us, just as you see and hear today.

ACTS 2:33

We take so much for granted every day . Health, eyesight, senses, ability to think, even the Trinity. Maybe especially the Trinity. God isn't a genie. Instead of asking for things, I need to spend time just saying "Thank you"- even just for the beauty of a sunset!

Dear God; Do not let me take the Holy Spirit or Jesus or You for granted. Amen.

*

March 16th
And the Lord said to them, "Now listen to me! Even with the prophets, I, the Lord communicate by visions and dreams."

NUMBERS 12:6

While I was having priority problems, I spent most of my time rebuking Satan. Trapped by the lie that I was "never" going to be able to get my priorities straight, frustration became depression, which dragged me down. Then one night, I had a dream. The thing that was threatening to take top priority in my life appeared to be shrinking! I woke up so happy. It was as if God was right there in the room and had said, "Hang in there, Gal. Little by little." Since then there have been many other dreams from God (isn't it nice to know that not all dreams come from five-alarm chili eaten before bedtime, or the kid's video we saw for the zillionth time that day? We may never sleep again!) with similar messages. It is nice to know that we are so loved.

Dear God; Help me to recall last night's dreams so I will know what You are telling me to do. Amen.

*

March 17th
My sheep know My voice. I know them and they follow Me.

JOHN 10:27

It truly amazes me how and when I hear from Him. When I'm in the middle of something He wants me to stop doing, I sense it immediately. When I'm worried or fearful, I get a warm feeling of peace spreading over me. Or when "something tells me" to look up in the sky at the beauty He wants to show me. Sometimes I can even sense Him saying "hello" or "good morning". I hope Jesus loves hearing from me as much a I love hearing from him.

Dear God; Your voice is sweet and melodious to my ears and wonderful to my heart. Help me not stray from you. Amen.

*

March 18th
Don't let people waste time in endless speculation over myths and spiritual pedigrees.

1 TIMOTHY 1:4

There has been so much discussion over "religion" and who has the right doctrine over the years. It is getting less and less nowadays. Thankfully. Although Jesus was a Jew, He came to free all of us. No matter what Christian religion we practice, we all worship the same Jesus (or we could not call ourselves Christians in the first place). God never meant for His people to argue over how to worship Him. He just wants our love, not our doctrine. He doesn't care how we worship Him, as long as we do.

Dear God; Help me walk away from "religious" discussions. Amen.

*

March 19th
The Lord is God, shining upon us. Bring forward the sacrifice and put it on the altar.

PSALM 118:27

Lifestyle changes bring about sacrifice. It's easy to say that we're going to put God first. When it's time to line the things we hold dear (here in the natural) up on the altar and set fire to them, it becomes more difficult. Some of us struggle with this more than others. For some, letting go is easy. Others of us battle for months and even years. But then it wouldn't be much of a sacrifice if it was something we wanted to give up, would it?

Dear God; Help me remember that anything that takes my full attention from You is sin, and should be gotten rid of. Shine on the things I need to see more clearly, that you want me to get rid of. In Jesus' name. Amen.

March 20th

For every house has a builder, but God is the one who made everything.

HEBREWS 3:4

I remember when I was about four years old I asked my adult neighbor if he knew who made my tricycle. He launched into an explanation about manufacturers and factories that was way beyond my years. Finally, I interrupted with, "God made it because He knew that I'd like it!" I happily rode off on my trike that God created just for me.

Dear God; I thank You for everything I can see and/or name. Amen.

*

March 21st

I am one witness, and My Father who sent me is the other.

JOHN 8:18

We are to be witnesses of His. He is the only One who has ever seen Heaven, yet has walked on earth. There are images scattered throughout the New Testament of Heaven, yet we really cannot grasp the splendor and the beauty awaiting us.

Here on earth, His artistry is so beautiful. All we have to do is open our eyes to it. I like to think of it as "the coming attractions" shown in movie theatres, just like a sneak preview.

Dear God; You and Jesus are the only witnesses of our Home. Help me live so that each day I get a step closer to You and Home. Amen.

*

March 22nd

So God created people in His own image; God patterned them after himself; male and female He created them.

GENESIS 1:27

I used to wonder how it could be that we are created in His image. We come in various sizes, shapes and colors. Even within families, siblings can look and be so different from each other. Now I think it's because we're all the same race, the human race, and we who call ourselves Christians have Jesus in our hearts, that we project His image. I hope my thoughts, words, and deeds do him Justice!

Dear God; Help me to lead my life to let others know that I am truly Your Child. Amen.

*

March 23rd

In its place you have clothed yourselves with a brand-new nature that is continually being renewed as you learn more and more about Christ, who created this new nature within you.

COLOSSIANS 3:10

When I was a little girl, I used to play with my Mom's clothes and jewelry, and pretend all sorts of scenarios about the "grown-up lady" I'd someday be. Eventually, I grew into those clothes. As I am devouring books galore to learn about Him, I have peace within me, because I know that I will eventually grow into "this new nature" and it will be custom-made to fit just perfectly by His divine will.

Dear God; I excitedly inhale book after book about You and how to live for You. When I look back at who I used to be, I barely recognize myself (and gratefully so). Amen.

*

March 24th

Hatred stirs up quarrels, but love covers all offenses.

PSALM 10:12

I don't understand "hate groups" (and I pray that I never do) How can people spew hate all the time? In literature that they print up, streams of hate comes by words and that leads to actions. How can people have that much hatred inside of them? The worst part is that the hatred is passed down from generation to generation. How do you look into the big, trusting eyes of a child and teach him or her to hate? Hate is like a poison that eats away at all vessels that contain it. It takes them from beautiful vases to the vilest of dumpsters. I'd rather be a vase. That's why humans were created to love each other like He taught us.

Dear God; Help me to show love to everyone and in every situation. Hatred is never worth the waste of energy. In Jesus' name. Amen.

*

March 25th

Don't be impressed with your own wisdom. Instead fear the Lord and turn your back on evil.

PROVERBS 3:7

Some days all I seem to do is rebuke demons. I feel like one of those comic book heroes from my childhood complete with onomatopoeia (spelling out of a side-effect) bubbles, that is punching her way through a line of "baddies". If I turn my back, they are in my face, if I turn my face away, they are at my elbow. I'm just glad He's inside of me to keep me safe.

Dear God; Help me to say "Get thee behind me, Satan" as often as I need to. Thank you. Amen.

*

March 26th

A cheerful heart is good medicine, but a broken spirit saps a person's strength.

PROVERBS 17:22

While working on this book, I had a medical test. The side effects put me in bed, flat on my back, for four days. (My bedroom ceiling doesn't even have tiles with holes in them so I could count them.) Although I was bored to death and not too happy about it, once I stopped spending my waking moments obsessing over every little symptom, I got better. It was then that I could get on with my life (and this book). All it takes is the proper focus.

Dear God, A smile, a laugh should be bottled. A positive attitude is by far a better cure-all than a constant stream of complaints. Staying "up" means staying energetic and peaceful. Help me fight the symptoms of chronic fatigue syndrome with attitude. In Jesus' name. Amen.

*

March 27th
Keep on praying.

1 THESSALONIANS 5:17

I admire those who pray constantly. I mean about everything, anywhere, anytime (all the time). I'm trying. I'm really trying. It's also easier, at least for me, to ask for things for myself (I'm ashamed to admit) than intercessory prayer or just fellowshipping with Him. I realize I have a long way to go, but I am ready to enjoy the journey.

Dear God; Teach me to make praying just like breathing. Thank you. Amen.

*

March 28th
You will be blessed wherever you go, both in coming and going.

DEUTERONOMY 28:6

Whenever I think about how many blessings I have, I almost get giddy. It's true that I am blessed as I go in my house and come out of my home. Everywhere I look, He is blessing me. A roof over my head, food on my table, a real bed to sleep in. Blue skies, roses budding by my back deck, soft clouds. God blesses each of us with the good life, all we have to do is look for it. It's whatever we make of it.

Dear God; Remind me that Your blessings always cascade on me. Amen.

*

March 29th
...But first let's find out what the Lord says.

2 CHRONICLES 18:4

"What do you think?" became my favorite question when I was in my teens. I used to make my decisions after spending hours on the phone with friends, searching for the reader write-ins of the teen and fashion magazines, asking favorite teachers, and as a last resort, my parents. No matter how good the advice seemed I always ended up in the middle of a mess. It was so simple, all I had to do was ask Him first and then I didn't have to seek any more opinions. His is the only one that every really matters.

Dear God; No matter how big or small the problem, help me bring it to You first for Your guidance and blessing. Amen.

*

March 30th

And I know it is important to love Him with all my heart, all my understanding and all my strength, and to love my neighbor as myself. This is more important then to offer all of the burnt offerings and sacrifices required in the law.

MARK 12:33

Isn't it funny that we count the days down to Easter because we can't wait to go back to whatever it was that we gave up for Lent (usually sweets)? I've decided that instead of sacrifices that are pretty meaningless (except to help drop some pounds), I am going to make a lifestyle adjustment instead. I'm going to adhere to this commandment with all I've got, like my life depended on it - because it does.

Dear God; Instead of saying what I won't do this Lenten season, let me pledge to love You as Your word says. Amen.

*

March 31st

Not that I was ever in need, for I have learned how to get along happily whether I have much or little.

PHILIPPIANS 4:11

My late maternal grandmother used to aggravate us at gift-giving occasions because she insisted she didn't need anything (she never used the word "want".) She kept appliances until smoke came out of them, she wore clothes until they fell off of her, kept things like linens until they were thread-bare. She had been raised in a poor environment. I was raised in a middle-class home, the beginning of the "more" generation where new things have been bought "just because". I'm only now starting to appreciate the "make do" mentality. Actually, it's more of a "counting-your-blessings" mentality. What I have, little to some, much to others, is only because it is what He has blessed me with, and wants me to have at this time in my life.

Dear God; I will strive to be content with what I have instead of giving in to the false god of "more". Amen.

APRIL

April 1st
For as Jonah was in the belly of the great fish for three days and three nights, so I, the Son of Man, will be in the heart of the earth for three days ad three nights.

MATTHEW 12:40

When I think of April, I always think of Easter and the miracle of the Resurrection. What would life be like if Jesus hadn't died and risen for us? I simply can't imagine it. I also don't know how people living without Jesus get through a single day. Putting Jesus first in our lives can be a real struggle, but look what He did for us.

Dear God; Easter brings the greatest miracle of all. Let me keep my Easter joy all year. Thank You. Amen.

*

April 2nd
When I am raised to life again, you will know that I in My Father, and you are in Me, and I am in you.

JOHN 14:20

Jesus is alive! There is no past tense where God is concerned. When we are "saved", we ask Jesus to live in our hearts. I struggle sometimes in putting Him first, but then I realize that He is in me, and it makes it easier. I only hope my face reflects His and that I look at the world through His eyes.

Dear God; Your Son was raised to life to live always in my heart. Amen.

*

April 3rd
And praise Him for demonstrating such unfailing love to me by honoring me before the king, his council, and all these mighty princes! I felt encouraged, because the gracious hand of the Lord my God was on me...

EZRA 7:28

When I was a pre-teen, there was a TV show on about three brothers in the late 1800s Pacific Northwest. To show his concern and affection for the youngest brother, the oldest brother would place both hands on the boy's shoulders. I always wished that there was someone to do that for me. Then I got older and realized that there is, Jesus. He is our "big brother" who will run to our rescue when we need it most, and just hang around to love us the rest of the time.

Dear God; You are my encouragement whenever and however I need it (even when I'm not aware that I do). I will pay close attention so I can feel Your hands on my shoulders. Amen.

*

April 4th
...O Lord, God of heaven, the great and awesome God who keeps His covenant of unfailing love with those who love Him and obey His commands, listen to my prayer! Look down and see me praying night and day...

NEHEMIAH 1:5-6

I often wonder what He thinks as He looks down at His creation. Wars. Murder. Rape. Sexual Abuse. Strip-malls and office buildings going up on every plot of land available.

Pollution. Starvation, When I was a little girl, I was told that a friend or loved one could "watch over you from Heaven." How painful that must be for a loved one to see us hurting here on earth. Or do they see only that good that's coming from our hurts? Maybe that's how God can stand to see what has become of His creation.

Dear God; What do You see when You look down at me? I want to see myself as You see me to experience Your unfailing love even closer. Amen.

*

April 5th
Heaven and earth will disappear, but My words will remain forever.

MARK 13:31

Truth never dies. That's why the Bible is still the most precious possession a Christian can have. I keep one of mine in my nightstand. When I have sleepless nights, it's there to keep me company. I wonder how many zillions of people have been "kept company" by the Bible down through the generations. I wonder how many of the world's crises have been dealt with over an open Bible. How precious the Words that guide us all.

Dear God; Forever is a long time. I'm glad Your Words will last that long. Amen.

*

April 6th
For the glory of Your name, O Lord, save me. In Your righteousness, bring us out of this distress.

PSALM 143:11

Distress, whether physical or emotional (or both) is our inheritance from the Garden. Strength and the peace the ability to cope brings are our inheritance from Jesus. No matter how many lies the serpent tells you, don't believe any of them. Jesus said, "the Truth will set you free." Free from distress, from pain, from anything as long as we make eye contact with Jesus and keep our gaze locked on Him.

Dear God; No matter what aspect of Fibromyalgia is bothering me, I know that You will help me. All I need do is ask. I'm asking right now. You are a great Father. You let me know that I am a beloved child. In Jesus' name. Amen.

*

April 7th
The rain pours down from the clouds, and everyone benefits from it.

JOB 36:28

When I was a child, my family had a tradition of a big picnic on Memorial Day. Unfortunately, our "picnic" was held indoors sometimes, due to rain. My great-aunt would get all my cousins and me chanting "rain, rain go away, come again another day" (not that it did any good). We were too young to realize just how valuable rain can be. All we knew was it kept us from playing in the big yard with the grill in the middle. There is always good behind whatever "rain" He sends, whenever He chooses to send it.

Dear God; There is a saying, "it takes both rain and sunshine to make a rainbow". Help me to remember that there is good in everyone and everything. Amen.

*

April 8th
The commandments of the Lord are right, bringing joy to the heart. The commands of the Lord are clear, giving insight to life.

PSALM 19:8

Wouldn't life be simple if every human being lived his or her life by the The Ten Commandments? Since we threw God out of school we have a generation who have no clue what those even are (yet they know the 12 step program).

I can imagine God pacing in front of His throne, muttering, "there are only Ten. What is so hard for all of them down there to understand? There are only Ten! Easy to understand at that." It would be easier if we all believed in three little words, "God loves me".

Dear God; Your commandments are clear. All I have to do is really look at them with a heart that is crystal clear so I will want to obey You. Amen.

*

April 9th
I love your sanctuary, Lord, the place where Your glory shines.

PSALM 26:8

Sanctuary. Just the sound of the word makes me feel safe. I know that I am safe with Him in my heart. I pray that my eyes will reflect His glory, all day, every day. I want to be one of those people who are said to "brighten up a room just by entering it".

With my focus on Him, I can't go wrong.

Dear God; Let my heart be a sanctuary so Your glory can shine for all the world to see. In Jesus' name. Amen.

*

April 10th
Listen to my voice in the morning, Lord. Each morning I bring my requests to You and wait expectantly.

PSALM 5:3

"Wait expectantly" reminds me of our little poodle. Once he heard the garage door go up in the evening, signaling my Mother's homecoming, he would race to the door, and shift his weight from paw to paw in excitement. His eyes would stay riveted on that door. No amount of toys or food could distract him. No matter what, he was going to stand his ground until the door opened and Mom walked in to scoop him up in her arms and get happy "kisses". We used to joke that his tail was going to fall off from being wagged so much. That's the kind of Christian I strive to be.

Dear God; Teach me patience day by day. Let me wait on You and not give up, no matter how long it takes. Amen.

*

April 11th
God has made everything beautiful in its own time. He has planted eternity into the human heart, but even so, people cannot see the whole scope of God's work from beginning to end.

ECCLESIASTES 3:1

In today's world, it is imperative to look for the beauty in everything and everyone. God put it there. That's how we recognize the God in one another. We have to look for the good, even in the meanest person and the ugliest object. If we saw the good, we couldn't possibly treat them bad. And that's what leads to the "eternity" part.

Dear God; Help me live like I know about that eternity and like I want to share in it. Amen.

*

April 12th
You are a garden fountain, a well of living water, as refreshing as the streams from the Lebanon mountains.

SONG OF SONGS 4:15

After my grandmother died, my Mother and I inherited the family pictures. It was amazing to see that I posed near fountains or waterfalls from the time I was very little. When I was old enough to have my own camera, I took my own pictures of the fountains and waterfalls. Swimming is my favorite activity. It's just like Jesus, we get carried along by the current, and there is no negative impact.

Dear God; Cold, clear, clean, crisp water. It buoys the human body just as You do. Let me not take it for granted. Thank you. Amen.

*

April 13th
And the Spirit of the Lord will rest on him-the Spirit of wisdom, and understanding, the Spirit of counsel and might, the Spirit of knowledge and the fear of the Lord.

ISAIAH 11:2

I was raised in a denomination where the Holy Spirit was not emphasized. It is only through my own reading and study that I have discovered the Spirit for myself. We are to rest in the Spirit as He rests in us. He is like a cold drink of lemonade on a ninety-degree day. Knowing He is there to help is like seeing and tasting that lemonade on a long walk home in that ninety-degree heat. All we have to do is pray and we will be refreshed.

Dear God; Le me reflect on the Spirit. Let me feel His presence always. Amen.

*

April 14th
You will live in joy and peace. The mountains and hills will burst into song and the trees of the field will clap their hands!

ISAIAH 55:12

This sums up the way I think of Spring. When I was growing up, my Mom's twin sister (the outdoorsy-one) took me on plenty of hikes. I remember one time, at some nature preserve or other, coming out of the trees and woods into a beautiful sun-splashed field. The trees did seem to be clapping their hands to the wildflower's melody. It was a great feeling.

Dear God; Joy and peace are such awesome gifts. Let me never to forget to thank You for them. Amen.

*

April 15th
But blessed are those who trust in the Lord and have made the Lord their hope and confidence.

JEREMIAH 17:7

We all know what self-confidence is, but how about God-confidence? Someone once said that faith isn't believing He can, but knowing that He will. Because God doesn't always work in the "right- this -second", the enemy has his opportunity to sow seeds of doubt. We choose water and tend those seeds by our level of God-confidence. That's one level worth raising.

Dear God; Our trust in You has been well earned. In an ever-changing world, it is good to have a Constant to rely on. Amen and Amen.

*

April 16th
If we are living now by the Holy Spirit, let us follow the Holy Spirit's leading in every part of our lives.

GALATIANS 5:25

I befriended a young woman that seemed to have one crisis after another in her life. After getting to know her better, I had planned to introduce her to Jesus and lead her to the Lord. Then I would team her up with my Spiritual mentor so she could learn more about the Holy Spirit. This young woman cussed like a sailor, was in an adulterous relationship, spent money like it was water (but complained that she never had any money) and spent a lot of time bending her elbow at the neighborhood bar. One day I spotted her reading her Bible. Happy that someone else had introduced her to Jesus, I smiled at her and commented on the Bible. Her response both surprised and distressed me. She said that she was doing Sunday School homework. I asked how long she had been attending Sunday School, to which her reply was "all of my life. My father is a Minister." She went on to say that Jesus was aware of her lifestyle, but He forgave her because He understands that humans make mistakes.

Dear God; Because Fibromyalgia steals a chunk of "control", it can cause a big struggle. As long as the Holy Spirit is involved, how can we not give Him control, and give it gladly. Amen.

*

April 17th
For He does great works too marvelous to understand. He performs miracles without number.

JOB 5:9

I am a people-watcher. Especially, I love to see the faces of children. An ice cream cone brings wide, radiant eyes. A visit to the petting zoo brings delighted squeals (especially after an unexpected "kiss" from an animal.) The word "no" (which always has more syllables when they say it then when we do) brings the opposite of ice cream cones and petting zoos. Yet behind all of those faces is His greatest miracle of all.

Dear God; You are so awesome. Your word, Your works, Your miracles. Keep me making You and being Your likeness my priority. Thank You. Amen.

*

April 18th
I will bring that group through the fire and make them pure, just as gold and silver are refined and purified by fire...

ZECHARIAH 13:9

Purification can't be complete without lots of time and lots of pain. Patience isn't easy when we're growing up (especially since we first have to admit that we need to grow up at all) in Christ. But what else can we do except wait, trust and grow? The higher the heat, the closer we are to being "done". Only God knows when that is, but when the heat feels like it's turning up, we'll know He's at work.

Dear God; Fibromyalgia is our fire, it is the means through which we will be better people, better Christians.. Thank You, Father, in Jesus' mighty name. Amen.

April 19th
For I am the Lord your God, who stirs up the sea, causing its waves to roar. My name is the Lord Almighty.

ISAIAH 51:15

The first time I was at the ocean, I was ten. I walked along the shore, looking for shells, with the strict instructions to keep an eye on the unpredictable waves. Never had I heard such power. It even overpowered my Mother's strong voice, yet I knew she was there, and that gave me comfort.

Just like our Father does.

Dear God; Your waves roar, yet You speak to us in gentle whispers. Help my ears and heart be open to You today. Amen.

*

April 20th
They repay me evil for good and oppose me because I stand for the right.

PSALM 38:20

On April 20, 1999 (Adolf Hitler's birthday), two troubled teenage boys opened fire on their fellow students and teachers at Columbine High School. After it was over, the boys turned the guns on themselves, leaving fifteen dead (including themselves and one teacher) and many more wounded. Later, it was learned that some of the students died simply because they proudly admitted to believing in God. Martyrs are brave people. They did for Him what He did for them - gave their lives happily.

Dear God; Help me to call to mind the massacre at Columbine High School in Littleton, Colorado. Help me to have faith as strong as Rachel and Cassie who died because they believed in You. Amen.

*

April 21st
O Israel, can I not do to you as this potter has done to his clay? As the clay is in the potter's hand, so You are in My hand.

JEREMIAH 18:6

As we all know, being poked and prodded is no fun. Each new “crisis” is another whirl on the potter’s wheel. He knows what He’s doing. After all, God started the human race with a lump of clay. He’s going to keep working until we’re a work of art. He isn’t going to leave us lopsided (or a cracked pot, either). All we have to do is let ourselves be the clay and not try to be the potter (which is easier said than done.)

Dear God; Let me know that one more spin on the potter’s wheel is Your will for me. Help me have the patience to accept it. Amen.

*

April 22nd

Wait! Don’t hurt the land or the sea or the trees until we have placed the seal of God on the foreheads of their servants.

REVELATION 7:3

God created our world. That fact alone should make it precious to us so that we take care of it better. Because the earth has always been here, we really take it for granted. Take time to watch the new life that springtime brings, just outside the window. God wants us to be caretakers of His creation, and who are we to argue with God?

Dear God; Today is Earth Day. Help us be compassionate to the earth today but not forget it tomorrow. In Jesus’ name. Amen.

*

April 23rd

All around Him was a glowing halo, like a rainbow shining through the clouds. This was the way the glory of the Lord appeared to me…

EZEKIEL 1:28

When I was in my teens, my aunt took me to Niagara Falls. We even stayed on the Canadian side just so we could say we had stayed in a foreign country. While we were enjoying the various things to do there, the sun came out brightly. Because the Falls produce a constant mist, everywhere we turned there were rainbows. I lost count, there were so many. One was more beautiful than the one before it. I felt hugged by God that day, something I’ll never forget as long as I live.

Dear God; Let me never forget the significance of the rainbow. Amen.

*

April 24th
...People need more than bread for their life; they must feed on every word of God.

MATTHEW 4:4

Sometimes, when I'm not feeling well, or when I'm fatigued, it is easy for me to get lazy and procrastinate my Bible time. When I do get back on track, I realize just how much I need His Word. Like vitamin C to prevent a cold, the first robin of Spring, or a cool breeze on a humid night, the Word of God is all of that and more. No matter what translation or version, God's Word is precious and should not be ignored.

Dear God; The Bible is a feast in buffet style. I've got my plate and an insatiable appetite! Amen and Amen.

*

April 25th
Yet I will rejoice in the Lord! I will be joyful in the God of my salvation.

HABAKKUK 3:18

If my joy is missing, it's only because I allowed Satan to steal it. With this in mind, I am trying to keep a leash on my joy. Like a big helium balloon, if I don't hold the string tightly, off goes my joy. Sometimes it's easier for me to allow Satan to steal it than others. When my mind is on my salvation, and what He has done for me, my joy stays put.

Dear God; Salvation! What a delirious-sounding word. When I realize what Jesus willingly suffered for me, my Fibromyalgia pales by comparison. Let me show my joy always, Jesus. Amen.

*

April 26th
My heart is confident in You, O God, no wonder I can sing Your praises!

PSALM 57:7

When I was in 6th grade, I was thrown out of choir because I couldn't sing. This was a mandatory choir because I went to school there, school children from many grades had to belong to the choir. It was a devastating blow to my self-esteem (or lack there of), but since then I've learned that God doesn't care what I sound like (which is good, because I still can't sing) when I praise Him, as long as I praise Him.

Dear God; Confidence. That feels so good. Let me never stop praising You. Amen.

*

April 27th

But Lot's wife looked back as she was following along behind him, and she became a pillar of salt.

GENESIS 19:26

I don't know that we'll become pillars of salt, but I do know that there are consequences we all must pay if we don't heed the sound of His voice. I hope I will trust Him and listen to Him more than giving in to temptation, or the urge to disobey. Although I won't turn into a pillar of salt, I don't want to face those consequences. I love Him too much for that.

Dear God; When You've given Your Word over the centuries, You have kept it. Lot's wife is good example of that. I cannot imagine anyone not trusting You or testing You just to see "if He'll really do it". Let me trust and not test. Amen.

*

April 28th

And after the earthquake there was fire, but the Lord was not in the fire. And after the fire there was the sound of a gentle whisper.

1 KINGS 19:12

Why do we always expect such huge things, instead of the simple, small things already right h ere in all of us? I'd rather be whispered to than shouted at any day. I believe that He would rather whisper than shout, too. I just hope that when He does whisper, I'm not listening to "junk" and miss Him.

Dear God; Help me to stop expecting the earthquake when I already have the gentle whisper, all I need do is pay attention. Amen.

*

April 29th

But if you pray to God and seek the favor of the Almighty, if you are pure and live with complete integrity, He will rise up and restore your happy home. And though you started with little, you will end with much.

JOB 8:5-7

One of the jobs I have held was not noted for complimenting its employees. As a matter of fact, they were fast at dishing out the discipline, and the negative atmosphere was sometimes hard to take. The last evaluation I had brought a wonderful surprise. I was actually complimented on my integrity! That was only because I vowed to live my life for Him. That compliment was the "much" part of this.

Dear God; Let me use Your gift of integrity to the hilt. Let me be a happy, blessed, peaceful Christian. In Jesus' name. Amen.

*

April 30th

God blesses those who realize their need for Him, for the Kingdom of Heaven is given to them.

MATTHEW 5:3

Everyday in every way, I realize my need for Him. It seems that I need Him more and more as time goes by. I am only now realizing the power (and ease) of prayer, and that it can be done in virtually any situation anywhere I may be. I'm glad that He's "user friendly".

Dear God; I am so glad that You are there whenever I need You (which is constant) and I cannot imagine life without You. Thank You that I don't have to. Amen.

MAY

May 1st

The humble will be filled with fresh joy from the Lord. Those who are poor will rejoice in the Holy One of Israel.

ISAIAH 29:19

When I was a child, my favorite place to be was at my great-aunt's house. They lived all their lives, as it turned out, in the house they were born in. Their yard was double the space of most in the area, an acre, which was garden and fruit trees. To a little kid, it might as well have been a farm. I especially liked to help with the homemade applesauce (I was taste-tester). All of this was a long way that I liken "fresh joy" to that first wonderful taste of fresh applesauce.

Dear God; "Fresh joy" sounds so wonderful, even more than spring rain, or the juiciest produce. Let me be humble and poor, in Jesus' name. Amen.

*

May 2nd

Ears to hear and eyes to see - both are gifts from the Lord.

PROVERBS 20:12

How much we take for granted. Even though we have our maladies, we can still count our blessings. We each have something to be grateful for, something that we take for granted everyday.

Take the time right now to figure out what that is and say a special "thank You" to Our Father.

Dear God; Thank You for blessing me so much. Amen and amen.

*

May 3rd

He must become greater and greater and I must become less and less.

JOHN 3:30

Last night I had a dream. I was standing beside my own bed. My face was very large, but it shrank to tiny. Then it became God's face, but it stayed the same tiny size. This was His way of telling me that I was becoming less and less but He is not becoming greater and greater. God has always used dreams to communicate with me, and I got His message loud and clear.

Dear God; My plans, my "things", my finances, my career, etc., are all subject to Your will. In Jesus' holy name. Amen.

*

May 4th
My Spirit remains among you, just as I promised when you came out of Egypt. So do not be afraid.

HAGGAI 2:5

Fear comes in varying degrees and for various reasons. But is always inflated by the same hot air, our own imagination. Whether it is a new medical problem (and we have ourselves dead and buried twice over before we get to the doctor), a job interview (that the mind turns into an interrogation by a prison warden-type), or anything the mind can twist. (What a liar Satan is!) I'm glad we have the Spirit of our Comforter or fear would win out.

Dear God; Lead me out of my own Egypt. Let me walk on my own, don't drag me kick and screaming. Amen.

*

May 5th
I want you all to know about the miraculous signs and wonders the Most High God has performed for me.

DANIEL 4:2

There are four miracles in my life for which I am grateful, but are often taken for granted. One is my walker. It's a three-wheeler-fold-up model that allows me stability and mobility. Another is my computer (a must for a writer because it makes editing a breeze) because I can do so much with it. Next is my shower chair and spray head so I can do more for myself (and self-esteem). Of all the miracles in my life, my Mother, with whom I live, is my best and brightest. Not only is she my best friend, and sometime nursemaid, she is also chauffeur, chef, teacher, pupil, and all-around-good-sport (and great at board games, too). Do I sound happy? You bet.

Dear God; Help me to look for my everyday miracle. Amen.

*

May 6th
We can gather out thoughts, but the Lord gives the right answer.

PROVERBS 16:1

I must give God fits. I am one of those people who has to question "why", "when", and "how". I have wasted a lot of time trying to figure out what God doesn't want me to know yet or He would have revealed to me. If I just shut up long enough, I'll save myself a lot of problems, headaches, and time.

Dear God; Don't allow me to waste too much energy trying to figure things out before I turn to You. Amen.

*

May 7th
The Lord will guide you continually, watering your life when you are dry and keeping you healthy, too. You will be like a well-watered garden, like an ever-flowing spring.

ISAIAH 58:11

When I was about five or six, I was given a little flowerpot with soil and seed inside. Just add water. Foolproof, right? Not when you're an impatient five-or-six-year-old with access to a watering can. I must have watered it four times a day at least, unbeknownst to any adult in the house. Of course, the little flower didn't grown. It floated away. I'm glad He's better at gardening than I am.

Dear God; You are the supreme gardener. Thank You for caring for me the way a gardener cares for a delicate orchid. In Jesus' name. Amen.

*

May 8th
I will climb to the highest heavens and be like the Most High.
ISAIAH 14:14

I will never forget my first time riding on a mountain road. I was all of twelve years old and treated to a western vacation that summer. There were no guardrails on the winding roads, and because I was on the passenger side, I could see how steep those mountains really were. I was glad it wasn't winter and the roads icy. I tried my best not to look down, but the view was too spectacular. What an artist He is!

Dear God; Being like You is like climbing a mountain. Please don't let me look down so I quit climbing along my path. Help me keep going so I can keep growing. Amen.

*

May 9th
Fear of the Lord teaches a person to be wise; humility precedes honor.
PROVERBS 15:33

I never know what to say when someone asks "how are you?" Is the question there just to be polite? Is the asker really interested? How much do I disclose before it becomes a whiny complaining session that neither asker nor I want to hear? I like to keep it upbeat as much as I can, anyway. Maybe that's my little bit of wisdom after all.

Dear God; Humility sometimes can be tricky. Do I mention my Fibromyalgia and how I'm feeling so someone can gush how brave I am? Do I ask for help and maybe not appear so brave or do I struggle and maybe make a mess of things? Teach me to "be". Amen.

*

May 10th
Come, people of Israel, let us walk in the light of the Lord!
ISAIAH 2:5

It never ceases to amaze me. I have dusted off TV screens, changed to computer glasses, and wiped off mirrors before realizing that I'd see better, if only I would clean my glasses! I've worn glasses since I was six. You'd think I'd have learned by now. I've spent a lot of time not seeing my best. Now I'm finally wising up. What I really want more than anything is to see Him as clearly as possible. I'm doing all the maintenance I can so I can see Him my best.

Dear God; Let us walk in Your Light so that we can see You clearly! In Jesus' name. Amen.

*

May 11th

You must crave pure spiritual milk so that you can grow into the fullness of your salvation. Cry out for this nourishment as a baby cries for milk.

1 PETER 2:2

The first thing newborns seem to react to is the hunger sensation. The second seems to be the scent of milk. Some babies teethe on hymnals in the pews at church. As baby Christians, we all learn everything else by reading His Word. We mature by the amount we put into application in our lives.

Dear God; I cry for You. I cry for Your Spirit. Satisfy my cravings to that I am not tempted to satisfy them by the world. In Jesus' name. Amen.

*

May 12th

Make me walk along the path of Your commands, for that is where my happiness is found.

PSALM 119:35

When I'm out, the faces of people really strike me. From the harried young mother with the tiny toddler by the hand, to the teenager on the cell phone, to the business person with the brief case who keeps looking at his watch. No one looks peaceful or happy. When will people realize that happiness comes from within? More specifically, within the Word of God. It makes me happy to imagine Him smiling down at me when I truly live for Him.

Dear God; Let me always find my happiness in You, steer me away from the world. Amen.

May 13th
The water glistens in its wake. One would think the sea had turned white.
JOB 41:32

This is another of those wonderful "miracles". When we go to visit my aunt and uncle in Florida, you'll find me sitting on their terrace as I watch the sun reflect off the water floors below. When boats or wave runners go by, the sun off the white waves is almost blinding. Yet I can't tear my eyes away. That's the way it'll be when we see Him; blinding, but we won't be able to tear our eyes away.

Dear God; Thank You for all the images of water in the Bible. It is water, after all, that keeps us alive. Amen.

*

May 14th
I could have no greater joy than to hear that my children live in the truth.
3 JOHN 1:4

As a little girl, at punishment time, I was told to "go stand in the corner and tell Jesus you're sorry. When you act like that, you make Him cry." It devastated me. Every time I know I have gone against Him I think of that reprimand. Because I am so happy in Him, I want Him to be happy with me.

Dear God; Let me return to the joy You have given me by abiding in Your truth. Amen.

*

May 15th
Instead, there must be a Spiritual renewal of your thoughts and attitudes. You must display a new nature because you are a new person created in God's likeness - righteous, holy, and true.
EPHESIANS 4:23-24

Renewal of thoughts has been my biggest challenge as a Christian. While my thoughts aren't dirty or "bad", they are judgmental and a can be a waste of time. I've spent a lot of my life daydreaming, "lost in thought". I'm really trying to bring this to His obedience. How do you stop yourself from thinking? Someone should invent a "brain-purifier" to strain out all the bad stuff and leave in all the good, like a water-purifier.

Dear God; When someone compares someone else to a parent, grandparent, or sibling (to their better qualities) it is quite a compliment. Let me not only live so that I can be compared to You (and make You proud), but let me see You in others. In Jesus' name. Amen.

*

May 16th

So you received my message with joy from the Holy Spirit in spite of the severe suffering it brought you. In this way, you imitated both the Lord and us.

1 THESSALONIANS 1:6

It seems like joy and suffering go hand-in-hand. They seem to follow each other like shadows. I believe Jesus was as joyful (although the Bible never says He smiled or laughed) as sorrowful. Both of those are the way to be like a mirror to Jesus. What a big responsibility Our Father has given us.

Dear God; When we, Your Fibromyalgia patient/children suffer, it can be intense. But our suffering is nothing compared to the nails driven through His hands and feet as Your Son suffered on the cross for all of us. If we can only keep this in mind, our tears of pain will become tears of joy. In Jesus' name. Amen.

*

May 17th

For the sinful nature is always hostile to God. It never did obey God's laws and it never will.

ROMANS 8:7

God was hurt, I'm sure, when Adam and Eve fell. Having to send them out of the Garden was probably painful for Him. I feel bad when I know I've let someone down. When that Someone is God, I feel even worse. My natural man is dead, so why am I still grappling with him? There will always be a battle between the sinful and Spiritual natures. It's up to us to decide who wins.

Dear God; I ask not to be hostile to you. In Jesus' name. Amen.

*

May 18th
...Listen to me. Keep silent and I will teach you wisdom.

JOB 33:33

To lull myself to sleep, I bought a "sound ball" that plays various sounds for a half hour. It does the trick. One day, it dawned on me that I really wasn't hearing from God. I couldn't understand it. After all, I'm right here. But so are the stereo, TV, alarm clock, telephone, etc., that all make some sound. I realized that He isn't going to waste His time shouting when others are willing to hear Him whisper. Now, I try to spend at least one or two hours a day in as much silence as possible so I can hear and obey His voice.

Dear God; Lord, help me to shut up so I can hear Your voice. Thank You. Amen.

*

May 19th
Remember what happened to Lot's wife!

LUKE 17:32

Remember all the little things your mother said to you when you were a kid? Things like, "I hope you have kids like you when you grow up!" It isn't exactly a guilt-trip, but it was meant to let you know that you were giving your mother fits, and the ground you were standing on was getting shakier by the minute. The same is true of this reminder from Our Father. He is always in control, always. Just the way I like it.

Dear God; You are good and awesome, and still in control. Amen.

*

May 20th
For the life of every living thing is in His hand, and the breath of all humanity.

JOB 12:10

He is the Creator of all things. One lump of clay and a big breath started everything. Every illustration, metaphor, etc., that was ever used for Him is right on the mark, but it misses by so much because God is too awesome for anything but our obedience.

Dear God; You breathed life into us in the Garden. Like a lump of clay in the palm of Your hand is our world! You are constantly shaping that world and each one of us. Thank You. Amen.

*

May 21st

The young women will dance for joy, and the men - old and young-will join in the celebration. I will turn mourning into joy. I will comfort them and exchange their sorrow for rejoicing.

JEREMIAH 31:13

The biggest "trick" we have in our repertoire is that we can rejoice through our sorrow. Dwelling on doom and gloom (no matter what it is) does no one any good (except, maybe, Satan, who strives to keep us, and those around us, miserable).

God made us to have joy always. I'm not about to let Satan steal mine. God knows when we are hurting, but His joy is giving so it will sustain us, buoy us up, and we should not look a gift-horse in the mouth.

Dear God; I'm going to strap on my dancing shoes. Fibromyalgia causes enough grief. I am going to dance with joy (figuratively if not literally) for what abilities I do have. Thank You. Amen.

*

May 22nd

Your eye is a lamp for your body. A pure eye lets sunshine into your soul.

MATTHEW 6:22

Sunshine in our soul. What a wonderful statement. I love to sit outside on warm, sunny, days, and feel the sun through my shirt. I've all but fallen asleep out there, any number of times. There's just something about sunshine that makes me feel great, and makes me want it around all the time.

Dear God; Let me keep my eyes pure so I can keep the "sunshine in my soul". In Jesus' name. Amen.

*

May 23rd
For the wicked will be destroyed but those who trust in the Lord will possess the land.

PSALM 37:9

It never fails to surprise me at what we already have just by God's own promises and words. We struggle so to receive blessings, and get out of bondage when we can already do both just by reciting verses from the Bible. So why don't we read and absorb as much as we need to stand firm?

Dear God; Help me to tie a knot in the end of my rope and hang on. I want to live so that I not only get my inheritance, but that I finally deserve it. In Jesus' name. Amen.

*

May 24th
...Amen! Blessing and glory and wisdom and honor and power and strength belong to your God forever and ever. Amen!

REVELATION 7:12

Everything we try to find through an overabundance of food and techno-toys is listed in the Bible as being in God. We struggle so hard to buy our way to what God has already provided for us free of charge. All we have to do is go to God and He'll do the rest. Yet how many of us bang our heads on the wall in frustration all the because we don't have "it" (the hottest, biggest, newest, "best", etc.), nor do we realize that ones who do have "it" have a higher suicide rate, and bigger headaches than we can ever imagine. I'm sticking with God and He wants to give me.

Dear God; Please share the wealth. Thank You. Amen.

*

May 25th
So be strong and take courage, all you who put your hope in the Lord.
PSALM 31:24

I believe that strength comes from courage and courage comes from hope. They're all intertwined and they all come from God. I believe that when Adam and Eve sinned and fell, God knew that we would need something to rely on day after day to keep us going, so He kept that something in Himself and called it "hope'. If we lose sight of that we lose sight of everything.

Dear God; I am going to accept strength so I can rise above my Fibromyalgia and take Your courage to share with others so I can bless them. If I do this often enough, it will become habit. Amen.

*

May 26th
...Jesus stood and shouted to the crowds, "If you are thirsty, come to Me! If you believe in Me, come and drink! For the Scriptures declare that rivers of living water will flow out from within."
JOHN 7:37-38

Everyone walks around with bottles of water. If we become dehydrated we could well (no pun intended) die. We can't live without water. Jesus knows that. The Father made us that way on purpose. That's why there is so much imagery of water in the Bible. That's why He uses it to talk about Himself. We cannot live without Him anymore than we can live without water.

Dear God; You are everything I could ever possibly want or need. Amen.

*

May 27th
It is better to live humbly with the poor than to share plunder with the proud.
PROVERBS 16:19

When will we learn? If we "can't take it with us", or barter our way into heaven with it, why place such importance on it? There is One Name to be exulted, but it is not the name of this year's hot, new fashion designer emblazoned across a t-shirt. There is a lot to be said for the simpler lifestyle.

Dear God; Thank You for the gift of humility. I realize that my priorities in life are such that I come in dead last. Please make sure I stay last. Amen.

*

May 28th

I know the Lord is always with me. I will not be forsaken, for He is right beside me.

ACTS 2:25

Take time to feel His presence. This is something we all need. Take time to walk in stride with Him. Not only does He choose our path, but He also walks it with us so we won't stumble. He doesn't just throw us in the lake and hope we swim to safety. He catches us, gives us pointers on better swimming strokes, and He is right beside us to make sure we aren't in over our heads.

Dear God; Let me never forget this verse and never stop sensing it. Amen.

*

May 29th

I will put my Spirit in you, and you will live and return home to your own land. Then you will know that I am the Lord. You will see that I have done everything just as promised. I, the Lord, have spoken.

EZEKIEL 37:14

We've all been hurt by a broken promise in our day. That's because we put our trust everywhere but in Him. God will never break a promise because it is impossible for Him to do so. Not only is He the founder of our love walk, He is love. Our human minds can't comprehend the kind of love He has for us because humans are incapable of giving that type of love. All we can do is bask in it, and give as much as we are truly capable in return.

Dear God; Let me hear Your words and realize that Your promises can never be broken. Amen.

*

May 30th
Get together and pray...

ZEPHANAIAH 2:1

Memorial Day. Officially, at least, even if it doesn't happen to fall on the day we observe it. Even if there is or was not a veteran in the family, we have seen enough tape footage of wars to appreciate those who serve and have served our country. Jesus gave us freedom, Veterans just help enforce it. Don't forget them or their families today.

Dear God; Let my own selfish prayers not keep me from earnestly praying with and for the others. Amen.

*

May 31st
If you sinful people know how to give good gifts to y our children, how much more will your heavenly Father give good gifts to those who ask Him.

MATTHEW 7:11

We all have wonderful gifts that Our Father has given us that we didn't ask for (such as health, family, friends, etc.), but just thinking about our gifts that we don't have yet simply because we haven't asked gives me chills. He knows all our needs and when the timing is right for us. Yet, He waits for us to ask.

Dear God; Let me appreciate the gifts You have given me and not take them for granted. Amen.

JUNE

June 1st
Oh, that we might know the Lord! Let us press on to know Him! Then He will respond to us as surely as the arrival of dawn or the coming of rains in early spring.

HOSEA 6:3

He can't wait to love us. He can't wait to bless us. I am "pressing on" to know Him by reading His word, attending Bible Study, and reading everything I can about Him. The times I spend with Him are the best, however.

Dear God; I am desperate to know You. I just can't get enough! Help me to realize that it is mutual. Thank You for loving me and for letting me love You. In Jesus' mighty name. Amen.

*

June 2nd
One that day, I will purify the lips of all people...

ZEPHANIAH 3:9

I get so tired of all the four-letter words that come from the mouths of every age and gender without so much as an eye-blink. Bombarded for a few decades now by movie and television dialogue, the world has a new way to express itself. It isn't His way. The sound of the crude humor and blue interjections turn His stomach, especially when His name and the name of His Son are used as curse words!

Dear God; Let the example of Christian lips influence the world. Thank You. Amen.

*

June 3rd
A dry crust eaten in peace is better than a great feast with strife.

PROVERBS 17:1

When I was little, My Mom and I lived with her mother, her twin sister, and their two teenage brothers. If there was any sort of tension around the table, crumbs of "leftovers" from the day that managed to sneak their way home somehow, it ruined even the most wonderful culinary experience. It just goes to show what is on the inside is far better than any exterior façade the world could ever create.

Dear God; Help me be peaceful because peace is better than anything on earth. It is a gift from Jesus. Amen.

*

June 4th
Look at the proud! They trust in themselves, and their lives are crooked, but the righteous will live by their faith.

HABAKKUK 2:4

The world screams for us to trust only ourselves. It makes fun of us, "Bible Thumpers". Yet, look at the "crooked" mess the world is in. We know where our trust belongs. The world can make fun of us all they want, but our faith is always firm and unshakable just like Him.

Dear God; Living by faith is never easy, but always well worth it. Let this thought stick in my mind no matter what may come. Thank You. Amen.

*

June 5th
Blind guides! You strain your water so you don't accidentally swallow a gnat, then you swallow a camel.

MATTHEW 23:24

Jesus dealt with so many hypocrites in His day. People then were more concerned with doing what their "religion" expected than what the Scriptures told them. Sadly, I have known people (and I'm sure we all have), who are involved in church work just because it makes them "big shots', but their personal lives are anything but Christian.

Dear God; Open my eyes to what I am swallowing so it is only what you want me to. Amen.

June 6th
Yes, I am the vine; you are the branches. Those who remain in me, and I in them, will produce much fruit.

JOHN 15:5

There is nothing prettier than a bowl of freshly ripened fruit. Fresh fruit still on the tree, the sun brightening its color, is another touch of His artistry. The challenge is living so our fruit equals His. For that, we must be pruned. He is the gardener. All we need do is let our fruit shine.

Dear God; Prune me so my fruit is always the best for You. Amen.

*

June 7th
Tune your ears to wisdom, and concentrate on understanding.

PROVERBS 2:2

Wouldn't it be something if life was like a radio? We could just pre-set a button and wisdom and understanding would come in crystal clear. Instead, what we choose as the background music of our lives does affect us. Have you ever been humming a song and not realize where it came from? Maybe piped into a store we were just in, or left on the car radio after the kids used it last night? It all affects our witness, if nothing else.

Dear God; Please don't let my ears be filled with static. I need You and I need to hear Your voice. Amen.

*

June 8th
The Lord replied, "Is it right for you to be angry about this?"

JONAH 4:4

People (even the ones going through it) don't realize there is more than the physical aspect involved in chronic illness. Although we should never dwell on it, the emotional aspect is also there. Especially when first diagnosed. Anger and resentment are present. If we give the whole thing to God right from the start, we have no reason to dwell on any aspect of life but the positive.

Dear God; Please help me not be angry with my Fibromyalgia when I need to nap and rest. Let me not see it as a waste of time. Thank You. Amen.

*

June 9th
Do for others what you would like them to do for you. This is a summary of all that is taught in the law and the prophets.

MATTHEW 7:12

I was raised by the Golden Rule before it became "do to others what they have already done to you." When I was in first grade, I "borrowed" my friend's hair band. I told my Mother that my friend gave it to me. Then when that failed (because the friend's mother called because the girl was frantic to find it), I insisted that I had borrowed it with permission. Then when I had run out of choices, I admitted to having pocketed it because it was my favorite, too.

After a lecture on not taking what doesn't belong to me, I went to my friend's house where I had to admit my crime, and apologize. On the way back home, I was asked how I would feel if someone took my things. That was the first lesson in the Golden Rule. I felt so badly about making my friend cry that it has always stuck with me.

Dear God; This verse should be a summary of how I live my life, my Christian witness. Amen.

*

June 10th
...The way to identify a tree or a person is by the kind of fruit that is produced.

MATTHEW 7:20

I always wanted to be a beautiful pine tree complete with pinecones. But because of my low self-esteem, I always saw myself as a little twig, without much growth. But now, after reading the Bible and realizing that God is the Love of my life, I see myself as a blossoming cherry tree. Sometimes, cherries can be sour, but I pray that mine are only sweet, and that He is pleased with them.

Dear God; Your Word is sunlight, water, and soil that helps my fruit tree grow. Let me produce only the best fruit for You. Amen.

*

June 11th
My heart has heard You say, "Come and talk with me", and my heart responds, "Lord, I am coming."

PSALM 27:8

Mastering the art of just talking to God hasn't happened for me, yet. I'm working on it, though. It's hard for me not to whine about something for myself, even when I'm doing my intercessory prayer list. I sort of get tongue-tied in His presence. "Hi, how are ya", doesn't seem appropriate somehow.

As I said, I am working on it. It's good to see this verse and know that He wants me to keep trying.

Dear God; Guide me on the path to You, and I'll get the hang of being conversational with You. Amen.

*

June 12th
I say to myself, "The Lord is my inheritance; therefore, I will hope in Him!"

LAMENTATIONS 3:24

Families have been torn apart by inheritances (or the fighting over them. Not just over the money, but the possessions, as well). Since I can't take Gramma's knickknacks with me, I'm glad to have His hope. Next to His Son, that's the best thing to keep in our hearts. It fits nicely, travels well, and is welcomed everywhere we could ever go.

Dear God; Hope is the best gift You could have given (beside Your Son, of course). Amen and Amen.

*

June 13th
The Sovereign Lord is my strength! He will make me as surefooted as a deer and bring me safely over the mountains.

HABAKKUK 3:19

Although our maladies zap our strength, He is there with an overflowing refill that will never run empty. Who else's hand could we ever imagine taking to guide us safely Home? When we get to Heaven, our bodies will be made whole and we will all be like pretty little fawns.

Dear God; Give me strength to do what I need to do. Thank You. Amen.

*

June 14th
You should keep asking each other, "What is the Lord's answer" or "What is the Lord saying?"

JEREMIAH 23:25

We all seek advice. Sometimes we seek it from our friends, family, or co-workers when He is the best Counselor around. Also, we give advice to friends, family, co-workers, that really should come from Him. Either way, seeker or giver, advice from the world can be confusing and destructive. Go to the Lord and send others to Him as well.

Dear God; Let me turn any advice-seeker to You. Don't let me give worldly advice that leads away from You. Amen.

*

June 15th
In that day, the Lord will end the bondage of His people. He will break the yoke of slavery and lift it from their shoulders.

ISAIAH 10:27

Everyone has some sort of bondage or other to give to the Lord. Since becoming born-again, He has broken a few off me and I have a few to go. (And I know they will go once they are in His hands.) Slavery to sin is the worst kind of slavery there is. It may take us awhile to let God have what needs to be lifted from us, but He will do it if we let Him.

Dear God; Help all my bondages be broken so I can replace them with You once and for all. Amen.

*

June 16th
The more words you speak, the less they mean. So why overdo it?
ECCLESIASTES 6:11

When I was two years old, I could recite the Lord's Prayer along with my ABC's. I wasn't praying nor was I ready to begin reading or spelling, I was just parroting back what my family said or sang to me. They were just a stream of words then. Now that I am an adult, I wonder how many times before I really knew Him that praying was just saying words? Reciting prayer isn't bad, as long as we aren't just talking to the wind.

Dear God; I am grateful that You and I have a relationship that transcends words. I can just be in Your presence. In Jesus' holy name. Amen.

*

June 17th
He floods the darkness with light; He brings light to the deepest gloom.
JOB 12:22

No matter how dreary and gloomy it seems, His light is always there. When the light are out, things become ominous, scary. That makes it ripe for the overactive imagination to sprout wings. Once He brings the light, there is never anything to fear again.

Dear God; As You bring light to the dark world, let me act as a prism to reflect Your light in my part of the world. Thank You. Amen.

*

June 18th
No one can serve two masters. For you will hate one and love the other, or be devoted to one and despise the other...
MATTHEW 6:27

Getting attention by the wrong means can become an idol just the same as money, alcohol, celebrities, or anything else we put in the slot reserved for Him in our lives. The term "master" is reserved for anything that we allow to control our lives, why not give our lives to the real "Master"?

Dear God; Fibromyalgia (and whining, complaining, self-pity, etc) can become an idol, but I will not let it take my focus from You. In Jesus' name. Amen.

*

June 19th
Their taunts pierce me like a fatal wound. They scoff, "Where is this God of yours?"

PSALM 42:10

God is always beside me and Jesus is in my heart all the time. I once heard a preacher say our faith should be such that someone could tell we're Christians just by looking at us (without Jesus pins or Christian slogans t-shirts). That's what I strive for. Any scoffers will have their answer even before they ask their question.

Dear God; Let me always feel Your presence beside and inside me so I can honestly answer "right here". In Jesus' name. Amen.

*

June 20th
The Lord is good. When trouble comes, He is a strong refuge. And He knows everyone who trusts in Him.

NAHUM 1:7

Isn't it great to know that there is somewhere we can run when we're under attack? How can we not trust Him? There are zillions (into infinity) of stories where those in trouble called to Him for help and were rewarded with sensations of peacefulness, and the knowledge that all would be well. How could we ever exist without this truth? Why would we ever want to?

Dear God; Who else can we go to in times of trouble that would make us feel so loved? I am glad You are there. In Jesus' name. Amen.

June 21st
What has God chosen for us? What is our inheritance from Almighty on High?

JOB 31:2

I believe that our inheritance is joy. We have the potential to be positive and to find our joy in every circumstance we face. Satan prowls around, his biggest mission is to steal our joy because he knows that it's like kicking the foundation out from under a building. That rest will come tumbling down.

Dear God; I love surprises and I can barely wait to see what awaits me in Heaven. Amen.

*

June 22nd
I lay down and slept. I woke up in safety, for the Lord was watching over me.

PSALM 3:5

There is nothing more precious than the sight of a little one asleep on Daddy's broad shoulder. Nothing says "trust" quite like it. "Warmth" and "safety" also come to mind.
As this earthly Daddy watches over his children, our heavenly Father watches over His Children. Isn't it great to know that we have the broadest shoulders of all to lean against when we need to?

Dear God; Asleep in Your arms with my head on Your shoulder, there is nowhere else I would rather be. Thank You. Amen.

*

June 23rd
They will neither hunger nor thirst. The searing sun and scorching desert winds will not reach them anymore. For the Lord in His mercy will lead them beside still waters.

ISAIAH 49:10

Still waters. Peace and tranquility. Food and water. He knows what we need - even before we do. We need to stop jumping the gun and trying to fulfill our own needs. We always make a mess of things, and now we're even worse off than we were before. If only we could visualize those still waters and just let Him provide us in His own time we would keep the peace and tranquility that Jesus gave us.

Dear God; You are our provider. Let me be still in Your presence. You know what I need. Amen.

*

June 24th

When He speaks, there is thunder in the heavens. He causes the clouds to rise over the earth. He sends the lightning with the rain and releases the wind from His storehouses.

JEREMIAH 10:13

Years ago, I worked in a department store. The employee lounge was down a rickety stairway that led to a musty hallway. Beyond the lounge was storage for the seasonal displays. One day, I ventured into the storage area. Although it was summer, glittering Christmas decorations met me. (I thanked the display person for not putting them up before the 4th of July!) Easter Bunnies with twinkling eyes hung above me. Valentine hearts, leprechauns, and patriotic displays waiting for their seasons were all around me. It was fun to see them all. God's storehouses for wind, rain, snow, and sunshine must be awesome - just like He is.

Dear God; Since You know what is appropriate for the weather, I can relax in the knowledge that You'll know what is right for me. Thank You. Amen.

*

June 25th

And it is good for the young to submit to the yoke of His discipline.

LAMENTATIONS 3:27

It is so important to teach the little ones discipline while they are still little. This becomes the foundation for their lives. Sometimes, when we first get out on our own, away from the eyes of all enforcing the rules, we go crazy and get into trouble. For some reason, we believe that we don't need rules. We need to follow His disciplines if we truly expect to live our lives for Him.

Dear God; Help me always remember the training of my childhood in all I do. Amen.

*

June 26th
For this is what the Sovereign Lord says, "I myself will search and find my sheep."

EZEKIEL 34:11

The Shepherd wants to herd His sheep-all of us, every last one. Sometimes I wonder if He hears us like sheep. Our recited words that are meaningless, our hollow promises to obey when nothing is further from our hearts, must sound like "baaa, baaa, baaa", to Him. We should strive to talk to Him, not bleat.

Dear God; I am here waiting to be found. In Jesus' name. Amen.

*

June 27th
He reveals deep and mysterious things and knows what lies hidden in darkness, though He Himself is surrounded by light.

DANIEL 2:22

For Him to overcome the darkness, He has to know something about it. The same is true for us. We cannot be victorious over Satan if we don't know that he is liar and a coward. We need to know something about him before we can guard ourselves from him. We also need to know about Him before we can live in His brightness. That is why reading His Word daily with an open heart is so very important.

Dear God; Help me see only Your brightness and light. Amen.

*

June 28th
...If any of you wants to be My follower, you must put aside your selfish ambition, shoulder your cross daily and follow me.

LUKE 9:23

Others have their own crosses to bear the same as we do. Our crosses get lighter as we focus on others with their crosses. Helping someone else balance his or her load means we have to let ours slip aside for a time. There is always ample time to shoulder our own crosses. Because He loves us, we follow Him by sharing that love with everyone else.

Dear God; Fibromyalgia is our cross. Sometimes where there is a chronic illness, it's hard not to focus inward. Help me to focus outward so I can truly be a follower. In Jesus' name. Amen.

*

June 29th
And He will be the source of our peace.

MICAH 5:5

Isn't it good to know that even though Satan is out to steal our peace, God has more than enough for every last person? Can you imagine the size of the locker marked "peace" in His storehouse? All we have to do is ask, and there it is for us. There is no "red tape" when it comes to Him, we can go right to the Source!

Dear God; When my supply runs out, help me go right to the Source. Amen.

*

June 30th
I love you, Lord; You are my strength.

PSALM 18:1

God is described as a "rock" in the Bible because at that time there was nothing stronger. There should be nothing stronger in our lives, either. Our love for Him, and His love for us, is stronger than anything man can create. We can never duplicate His strength, nor should we try. Just lean on the strength and rely on the love.

Dear God; When I get frustrated, weary, and weak due to the Fibromyalgia, I know that You have an extra supply of strength just waiting for me to ask for it! Thank You. Amen.

JULY

July 1st

Alcohol and prostitution have robbed My people of their brains.

HOSEA 4:11

The world's brains have been scrambled. It is apparent in movies, television (even cartoons and commercials), price tags, the worship of money and sex. I wish I could do something to change the world for God. Maybe I can. I can keep my mind focused on God and let my witness shine.

Dear God; Help me do what I can to take Your world back for You. In the mighty name of Jesus. Amen.

*

July 2nd

Even strong young lions sometimes go hungry, but those who trust in the Lord will never lack any good thing.

PSALM 34:10

We have as much as He wants us to at the time. All in His good time. He knows what we need (and the difference between our "needs" and "wants") and when we need it .

Everything God does is for our good. All we have to do is wait on Him to see the good take shape.

Dear God; When I think of everything You have ever done for me, how can I not trust You? Thank You again and again. Amen.

*

July 3rd

Being wise is as good as being rich; in fact, it is better.

ECCLESIASTES 7:11

It seems that the world has always thought too much of riches. The type of person under the portfolio and techno-toys is what He looks at. It's not what the world sees. Wouldn't it be something if we all banded together and blinded the world so they could see nothing else but what He sees?

Dear God; Let me list all the ways in which we can be rich other than financially. I'm sure I'll be awe-struck. Amen.

*

July 4th

Now, the Lord is Spirit, and where the Spirit of the Lord is, He gives freedom.

2 CORINTHIANS 3:17

We have the freedom of religion here in America. That's what our country was founded on. We can talk about Him, share Him through books and music, hear about Him from T.V. preachers, and not have to have Bibles smuggled to us. The freedoms we have here are nothing short of miracles.

Dear God; On that wonderful day in July 1776, the greatest freedom we received enables us to lift our heads high as we shout, "I'm proud to love Jesus." In His name. Amen.

*

July 5th

He delivered me from my powerful enemies, from those who hated me and were too strong for me.

Psalm 18:17

Nothing is too strong for us as long as we have Him. When it comes to buckling under to Satan and illness, my battle cry is, "Enough is enough! Get out of my way, my life is coming through!" I have no patience for temporary illness anymore because chronic illness is a full-time "job".

Dear God; Blessed is the realization that the only thing stronger than we are is You, God! This includes Fibromyalgia, and anything any demon in hell could possibly ever dream up. Thank you. Amen and Amen.

*

July 6th
Lord, You will grant us peace, for all we have accomplished is really from You.

ISAIAH 26:12

When I was a teenager, I befriended a girl my own age, who was in a wheelchair. At that point in my life, I focused on my inabilities and the negatives. Disco was just starting to gain popularity and my constant lament was that I couldn't dance. Tired of my whining, my friend, who was a paraplegic since birth, said to me one day, "Do you know what I would give to be able to do what you can do?" At my puzzled look, she continued, "I would give everything I have to be able to stand up out of this chair and take one step, just one, on my own." I learned not to take anything for granted after that.

Dear God; Help me remember that all I do is not only from You, but for You. Then I will surely have peace. Amen.

*

July 7th
But even so, the quiet words of a wise person are better than the shouts of a foolish king.

ECCELIASTES 11:4

Obnoxious commercials with loud music and even louder announcers, "heavy metal" music pounding so the entire neighborhood hears it while the vehicle vibrates and cell phones ringing out in questionable places (like church).

It's harder and harder to ignore the world all the time. But when our focus is in the right place, on God, it gets easier.

Dear God; Let me show that my mouth also has wisdom. Amen.

*

July 8th
Lord, You have brought light to my life; my God, You light up my darkness.
PSALM 18:28

God's light is everywhere. As we read His Word, a light bulb comes on. The path He leads us on is flooded by His light. Even turning on a lamp at night is from Him. Like flowers, we thrive in His sunshine. We were never meant to be in darkness.

Dear God; It's always darkest just before dawn. Let me look forward to that darkness because I know Your dawn will be so bright! In Jesus' name. Amen.

*

July 9th
So be very careful to love the Lord your God.

JOSHUA 2:19

A lot of us think we're so Spiritual! Is Christ really the center of our lives? We think He is until we go to the buffet line and stuff ourselves until our clothes no longer fit, or drool over the newest celebrity sensation, or skip Bible Study to hit the sales at the Mall. Then we need to sit down and take a long look in he mirror. Do we reflect Jesus or the world?

Dear God; It is one thing to love You, it is another to proclaim it all day long in thought, word and deed. Amen.

*

July 10th
When you obey Me, you remain in My love, just as I obey the Father and remain in His love.

JOHN 15:10

Obey. An easy word to pronounce; a tough thing to do. It's especially tough not to weigh the options, not to have to "think about it", to just say "yes" right away like He requires. Our choices are "smoking " and "non-smoking", and he isn't talking about cigarettes.

Dear God; Your example has taught me to be obedient. Let my example teach others obedience. In Jesus' name. Amen.

*

July 11th
Love does no wrong to anyone, so love satisfies all of God's requirements.
ROMANS 13:10

Everything that God has done for Bible heroes since the beginning of creation has been done out of love. Of course, the biggest was to give us Jesus.

Love shouldn't be something that is only done to a few people or at a certain time of the year. Is it so hard to say, "hello", or smile at a stranger, or assist someone in need? How can we say we live for God if we don't polish up our love walk until it shines like He does?

Dear God; Everything that You are or do starts and ends with love. Let me live all my days like that. In Jesus' name. Amen.

*

July 12th
The stone rejected by the builders has become the cornerstone. This is the Lord's doing and it is marvelous to see... For many are called, but few are chosen.

MATTHEW 21:42, 22:14

If I had a nickel for every time I was "chosen" last for anything in gym class from first grade until the day I graduated, I would be the wealthiest person alive. I dreaded those times, standing there like the idiot everyone professed me to be, waiting to walk to a team's side simply because I evened up the number of players. I wanted to be invisible. Jesus was hurt and rejected by an entire nation; all I had to worry about was an insignificant (on the grand scheme of things) class.

Dear God; Fibromyalgia has brought me a lot of rejection in my life. I identify with the cornerstone. Are You calling or choosing me? My answer is, "Here I am Lord, Right here. Amen.

*

July 13th
Satan, the god of this evil world, has blinded the minds of those who don't believe so they are unable to see the glorious light of the Good News that is

shining upon them. They don't understand the message we preach about the glory of Christ, who is the exact likeness of God.

2 CORINTHIANS 4:4

Crafty, cunning, able to make even the worst things seem attractive, cowardly and a liar. I could go on and on, but Satan isn't worth my time or energy. There is either darkness or light. They cannot co-exist. Everyday we are faced with the fork in the road. It's up to us which path we take.

Dear God; Let us rebuke Satan, who is bad news, so we can let the Good News shine through. Amen.

*

July 14th

And so the Lord says, "These people say they are Mine. They honor Me with their lips, but their hearts are far away. And their worship of Me amounts to nothing more than the human laws learned by rote."

ISAIAH 29:13

There are so many Christian denominations, each complete with its own "religious" beliefs. Slowly but surely, we are starting to accept each other's similarities and put aside our differences. Some Christians, no matter what denomination, are "pew dusters" on Sunday, and the rest of the week they act like they never heard of God! We need to be careful because the old cliché is too true: actions speak louder than words.

Dear God; Unfortunately, this rings as true in the world now as the day it was written so long ago. Let my heart belong to You. Help me get rid of legalism and seek to please only You. Amen.

*

July 15th

Please, Lord, prove that Your power is as great as You have claimed it to be.

NUMBERS 14:17

Only He can change me, and only He can change everyone else. We are all a "work in progress". We won't be finished until He has fine-tuned and polished us to His perfection.

No matter how hard we try, everything and everyone is only under His power. Prayer and patience are all we can offer.

Dear God; You and only You have the power to change me to be the person You want me to be. Amen.

*

July 16th
Peace and prosperity to you, your family, and everything you own.
1 SAMUEL 25:6

Prosperity isn't only measured by bank accounts or possessions. When we're successful, prosperous, we're happy, peaceful, and content. The people in our lives are better than any bank account. The joy we feel inside and give to others is the true symbol of our prosperity.

Dear God; Prosperity is Your gift to us. Help me to realize that it doesn't mean money only, as I have many ways to prosper. Thank You. Amen.

*

July 17th
Then hear from heaven, where You live, and forgive. Give Your people whatever they deserve, for You alone know the human heart.
2 CHRONICLES 6:30

He alone knows what is inside everyone. My judgment of others doesn't help Him one iota. He doesn't need my help ruling the world. We're so quick to make conclusions about others from the five-minute glimpse we get into their lives. How do they see us, using the same criteria?

Dear God; You know my heart. I pray that it will please You. Amen.

*

July 18th
Only three hundred of the men drank from their hands. All the others got down on their hands and knees and drank with their mouths in the stream.
JUDGES 7:6

When it comes to God, I want to be on my hands and knees, too. When I pick up my Bible, I don't want to ever stop reading. I am always impressed - and a little sheepish-about the great trust the Bible heroes showed for God. I want to lead others to also get on their hands and knees, just by my example.

Dear God; The ones that drank with their mouths in the stream were quenching their thirst for You. Help me never to drink from my hands again! Amen.

*

July 19th
I will never forget this awful time, as I grieve over my loss.
LAMENTATIONS 3:20

Can't there be a self-grieving period without spending the rest of our lives in a "pity-party"? I have known folks who have spent their entire lives playing "poor-little-me". The circumstances still apply whether we put it on the back burner or dwell on it.

The choice is ours. I find if I do the former, I can really enjoy myself despite anything negative in my life.

Dear God; Help me learn from my Fibromyalgia and from grieving for myself; the patience it creates in me, the strength it gives my character, etc., without throwing myself a "pity party". Amen.

*

July 20th
Long ago the Lord said to Israel, "I have loved you, My people, with an everlasting love with unfailing love I have drawn you to Myself."
JEREMIAH 3:13

Even though I am an adult, I still like to have my hand held during the bad times. God does that for each one of us. No matter what we do, not matter where we go, we can never get away from Him or His love. (Not that we would ever want to!) God always holds us to His chest to comfort us if only we let him.

Dear God; Your love is so awesome that I can't help but be drawn to You, even though I know I am not worthy to be near You. Thank You for calling me Your Child. Amen.

*

July 21st

The watchman replied "Morning is coming, but night will soon follow. If you wish to ask again, come back and ask."

ISAIAH 21:12

Morning is my time to talk to God (and thank Him in advance for all the good ways He'll bless me). I use a couple to kick the day off. Then I talk to Him as needed throughout the day. Night is my time to thank God for all the actual blessings of the day and spend time in intercessory prayer. If I can't sleep, I consider myself even more blessed because I have more time with Him.

Dear God; Chronic fatigue can cause us to dread mornings and/or nights. You cause us to hope and embrace our world. Let me hope in You always. Amen.

*

July 22nd

Choose a good reputation over great riches, for being held in high esteem is better than having silver or gold.

PROVERBS 22:1

If I ever overheard someone describe me in negative terms, I would be crushed. My Witness would mean nothing. I want to be known as honest and dependable. I don't like being lied to or disappointed by others. Maybe if I treat people well, they will reciprocate. What would really do me in, is if I overheard Him describe me in negative terms.

Dear God; When I give my word, Jesus, let my "no" mean "no" and my "yes" mean "yes". I am going to start to build up my reputation by standing behind my word. Most of all, I want my reputation to bring the words, "well done, good and faithful servant." Amen.

July 23rd

It is the Lord who provides the sun to light the day and the moon and the stars to light the night. It is He who stirs the sea into roaring waves.

JEREMIAH 31:35

One night I had a dream. I was waiting for someone to give me a ride home. I was on my late grandmother's front porch. The house was empty and I didn't have a key to get in. As darkness came, the porch light came on, but the porch railing became a jail cell and I had no way to get in or out, to contact anyone. He lights our way always, but gives us a way out, a way to follow Him without having to search too much for it.

Dear God; Thank You for lighting my way. Guide me safely in the right direction. Amen and Amen.

*

July 24th

The I will sprinkle clean water on you, and you will be clean. Your filth will be washed away, and you will no longer worship idols.

EZEKIEL 36:25

One of my favorite places to pray is in the shower. Just the water and body wash take my filth down the drain, the blood of Jesus washed me clean centuries ago. The world around us is a filthy place and I am so glad that I belong to His Kingdom instead. Idols are rampant in our world, with Satan behind each and every one.

Sometimes when I shower, I like to name the idols as the water washes them down the drain.

Dear God; Let me turn away from the idols of this world once and for all. Thank You. Amen.

*

July 25th

"Don't be afraid", he said, "for you are deeply loved by God. Be at peace; take heart and be strong!"...

DANIEL 10:19

We don't get stronger by lifting feathers! Never having to deal with anything unpleasant is a nice dream, but that's all it is. The Bible is there to help us plow through, not a guarantee that we can float over, not by any means. Fear is never necessary in Christianity, because we have Someone's strength to draw on if we ever run out.

Dear God; Your love brings me peace despite (of because of?) my Fibromyalgia. Amen.

*

July 26th
For though your hearts were once full of darkness, now you are full of light from the Lord, and your behavior should show it!

EPHESIANS 5:8

Our behavior as Christian Witnesses is called for right here. Light and dark don't just mean the position of the light switch. They don't just mean God and Satan. It means our attitude. It means our moods, our demeanor. Our Witness. We aren't to be phony about it, nor are we to walk around with big smiles plastered across our faces all the time. As we practice being Godly to others, it will become a habit that He endorses.

Dear God; Let me show the joy in my heart! In Jesus' name. Amen.

*

July 27th
...The wisdom we speak of is the secret wisdom of God, which was hidden in former times, though He made it for our benefit before the world began.

1 CORINTHIANS 2:7

The secret wisdom of God isn't so "secret", it's called "common sense". Book knowledge is fine, but if I don't have the wisdom to look before crossing the road, I'll end up as road kill just as quick as the uneducated squirrel. Wisdom is what leads us to treat others as we should, to love God as we should, to trust as we should, to "be" as we should.

Dear God; Help me to realize that prayer is the key to the secret. In Jesus' mighty name. Amen.

July 28th
Your children will rebuild the ruins of your cities. Then you will be known as the people who rebuild their walls and cities.

ISAIAH 58:12

When I was about six years old, I met my life-long best friend. We were so close. We called each other and/or visited every day f or hours, we said we were like the sister neither of us had. Then when she got married and had her first baby, we had a falling out. I don't even remember what it was about now. Anyway, we didn't speak again for fifteen years. She and her husband and son moved to a different part of the country, and although I thought about her often and prayed for her nearly daily (I was a Christian by then), I had no idea where she was.

Then one day I got a phone call. As soon as I heard her voice, I started to cry. She told me that she was now a Christian, too, and we talked for hours. But putting the friendship back together was tough. Trust needs to be in any relationship for it to even exist, and sometimes the tension between us was thicker than a brick. Although our lives have moved in separate directions (with often conflicting schedules), our friendship is back on track again. We're the same goofy kids we were, and we're still the sisters we never had.

Dear God; Help me realize that sometimes it takes longer to rebuild than it did to build in the first place. Help me have patience within myself. Amen.

*

July 29th
For God sent Jesus to take the punishment for our sins and satisfy God's anger against us. We are made right with God when we believe that Jesus shed His blood, sacrificing His life for us. God was being entirely fair and just when He did not punish those who sinned in former times.

ROMANS 3:25

Jesus gave us peace, and He was peace. A gift of a peace offering and our only change for salvation, that's Jesus. I believe that God's anger came out of disappointment in the world He created more than anything else. God used many, many sinners and outcasts in marvelous, miraculous ways, making them heroes of the Bible. By Jesus' blood, we can all be heroes, all we have to do is say "yes".

Dear God; Your Son has done what no one else could have ever done for me, for everyone. He was the human sacrifice, the human peace offering, to make everything right. Help me to keep that in mind as I face my world. In Your name. Amen.

*

July 30th
He will fill your mouth with laughter and your lips with shouts of joy.

JOB 8:21

Laughter is such great medicine. It costs less than any "miracle drug" around. If something happens and we think, "We'll look back on this some day and laugh", why not start "someday" right now? Laughing at ourselves is real wisdom. What comedians consider funny today is filth. Real humor is so spontaneous that it has no time for dirty jokes.

Dear God; Help me to realize that it's all about attitude. Attitude is everything. Let me live in joy and laughter. Amen.

*

July 31st
But the Lord still waits for you to come to Him so He can show you His love and compassion. For the Lord is a faithful God. Blessed are those who wait for Him to help them.

ISAIAH 30:18

Love, compassion, patience. One doesn't go far without the other. Waiting on the Lord does take an open heart as well as patience. Openness is the only way to serve Him. Our ears and minds have to be open, too, so we can hear and process what He tells us to do. All we have to do is stay willing to be His servant.

Dear God; I come to You with my heart - and patience - wide open. I want to stay in Your presence always. Amen.

AUGUST

August 1st
Truly, I love Your commands more than gold, even the finest gold.
PSALM 119:127

Even the finest gold can't be taken with us. That's why one of His commands is tithing. Saying "yes" to Him in all things is music to His ears, and is priceless to Him. Falling in love with Him means falling in love with His commandments.

Dear God; I have yet to see a church with stain glass windows depicting money, the world's obsession. Let us call to mind who we are to worship, and then let us do so. Amen.

*

August 2nd
Kind words are like honey - sweet to the soul and healthy for the body.
PROVERBS 16:24

It takes seconds to be kind, minutes to be rude. Sometimes it takes days, weeks or even months to let the rudeness boil up within. That isn't what God wants. The way to Heaven may very well start with what comes out of the mouth.

Dear God; If it takes less time to be kind than it does to be rude, help me to be a time saver!! In Jesus' name. Amen.

*

August 3rd
All night long I search for You; earnestly I seek for God...
ISAIAH 26:9

I love it when its dark and the air-conditioner is running so its cool in my room and I snuggle under the covers to talk God. That's when I tell Him my most hidden secrets (although they are not hidden from Him), sometimes putting them into words for the very first time. That's when it's the best, just God and me!

Dear God; Last night, as many nights with Fibromyalgia, I didn't sleep well. I used the time wisely. I spent it with You. I'm always amazed at how comfortable it feels in Your arms and how reluctant I am to ever feel any other way. Amen and Amen.

*

August 4th
At that time the Spirit of the Lord will come upon you with power, and you will prophesy with them. You will be changed into a different person.
1 SAMUEL 10:6

When I look back and see how far I've come, I know that I am a different person. Even when I look at pictures of myself then and now (even though hairstyle and color are the same - give or take a few gray hairs), I can see the difference. I never realized that I needed to change as much as I have, as much as I will. I like the new me much better, thanks.

Dear God; I look forward to my baptism of the Holy Spirit so I may speak in Your language. Amen.

*

August 5th
...It is the thought life that defiles you... All these vile things come from within; they are what defile you and make you unacceptable to God.
MARK 7:20,23

I've always been proud of myself when I've been able to shut myself up and just "think my share." But "thinking my share" is as wrong as saying it, especially when the thoughts are judgmental (like mine sometimes are). He knows our thoughts, positive or negative, and they do count.

Dear God; May every thought that registers with me be pleasing to You. Amen.

*

August 6th
Be strong and courageous! Don't be afraid of the king of Assyria or his mighty army, for there is a Power far greater on our side!
2 CHRONICLES 32:7

I love animals. I enjoy watching TV shows that tell all about animals. Every animal is especially designed for its environment. It has its own "equipment" (webbed feet, etc.), made just for it. I also enjoy looking at pictures of scenery. There are breathtaking pictures of sunsets and mountains. We can't look at our world and doubt God.

Dear God; I trust only in You so that I may indeed be strong and courageous. In Jesus' name. Amen.

*

August 7th
For in Him we live and move and exist. As one of your own poets says, "We are His offspring."
ACTS 17:28

Jesus called Him 'Our Father'. That makes us all brothers and sisters of Jesus Christ. It also makes us Princes and Princesses because Our Father is the King. We not only live for Him (we are Royalty after all) but because of Him. We exist because God created us.

Dear God; We cannot exist without You or our hearts. Let me keep You in my heart today so I can live and move in You. Amen.

*

August 8th
...Parents must not be put to death for the sins of their children, nor the children for the sins of their parents. Those worthy of death must be executed for their own crimes.
2 KINGS 14:6

The world today looks to blame past circumstances, environments, people (past, present, even total strangers) to blame for things that are wrong in our lives. Whether we dropped a glass and broke it, or we committed murder, there's always someone to blame. We blame everyone but ourselves. When we learn to shoulder the responsibility for ourselves, we'll be mature Christians.

Dear God; Part of becoming a mature Christian means taking responsibility on my own shoulders for my own acts. Let my actions only bring life and never cause death. Amen.

*

August 9th
...As surely as the Lord lives, I will say only what the Lord tells me to say.
1 KINGS 22:14

Whoever says that words don't hurt has never been verbally abused. Words can do as much harm as a belt or as much good as sunshine and rainbows. It's up to us to think before we speak. We are His mouthpieces who use His Word, and what He would have us say. In other words, Christians should talk like Christians.

Dear God; Let me think before I speak so that my words sound like Yours. Amen.

*

August 10th
Feel my pain and feel my trouble. Forgive all my sins.
PSALM 25:18

Sins don't cause illness or injury. Jesus took it upon Himself to die under the weight of our sins. They held Him on the cross as sure as the nails did. If He could handle all our sins, then he can handle all our problems today. Give all our problems to Him and see what He can do!

Dear God; My sins have not led to my Fibromyalgia (or any other illness). Your pain and trouble was a result of my sins. When my own pain and trouble threaten to overwhelm me, all I need do is remember what You did for me and because of me. In Your holy name. Amen.

*

August 11th
It is better to trust the Lord than to put confidence in people.

PSALM 118:8

Betrayal and disappointment never come from God, yet we always seem to go to friends and family with our problems, to seek advice, even to share "secrets" with. Sometimes, we're more trusting of humans than of God, but we wonder why we get hurt.

Just go to God in the first place, no matter what, because He would never hurt us.

Dear God; I trust You with my life because You are my life. You made my life. You know me better than I know myself. Help me lead my life so that You are proud of me. Help me to always place my trust in You and You alone. Amen.

*

August 12th
Now Joshua, son of Nun, was full of the Spirit of wisdom, for Moses had laid his hands on him. So the people of Israel obeyed him and did everything just as the Lord had commanded Moses.

DEUTERONOMY 34:9

My Spiritual mentor has answered questions, recommended TV preachers, helped with difficult Bible verses, and just been there when I needed her. She's become a very special person to me. I only hope that He sees fit to allow me to do this for someone else.

Dear God: You have blessed me with a Spiritual mentor. Let me pass the blessing along to someone else. In Jesus' mighty name. Amen

*

August 13th
...Call the citizens together for fasting and prayer...

1 KINGS 21:9

I make Daily Resolutions, they are easier to keep. I know my penchant for procrastination, so I ask God's help in keeping me on track.

Dear God; In my prayer time, let me know what I need to fast from; impulse buying, gossiping, worrying, "pity party" etc., and give me the strength to be without it. In Jesus' name. Amen

*

August 14th

He made the earth by His power, and He preserves it by His wisdom. He has stretched out the heavens by His understanding.

JEREMIAH 51:15

What awesome power God has. Can you imagine saying the word "dog" and having a real live dog appear on your lap? Or going out to the garage and saying "car" and having one appear? His wisdom keeps the planet turning, seasons passing, minutes clicking by silently. How are we repaying Him?

Dear God; You are so awesome, such a wonderful Creator, that all You had to do was speak things into existence. We cannot fathom Your wisdom or Your understanding. All we can do is keep You in our hearts and at the helm of our lives. Amen.

*

August 15th

For when two or three gather because they are Mine, I am there among them.

MATTHEW 18:20

God is with each individual, watching over us like a good Father. When people pray together, it makes our voices that much stronger. (They don't call them prayer "chains" for nothing, you know.) He loves to look down and see us congregated in His House and loves to hear the songs we lift to Him also, as well as our own individual prayers.

Dear God; You are here, no matter what or when. It becomes even more special when others are involved in prayer with us. Help remember to pray for those "others". Amen.

*

August 16th

But be very careful to obey all the commands and the laws that Moses gave to you. Love the Lord your God, walk in all His ways, obey His commands, be faithful to Him, and serve Him with all your heart and all your soul.

JOSHUA 22:5

We can't obey the commandments if we don't know what they are. We can't follow his path if we don't know where to find it. If He is a stranger to us or Someone we never get to know well, it isn't very likely that we'll even want to obey Him at all.

Dear God; How may I serve you? Let me bury Your Word in my heart. Amen.

*

August 17th

Rejoice, you people of Jerusalem! Rejoice in the Lord your God! For the rains He sends are an expression of His grace. Once more the autumn rains will come, as well as the rains of spring.

JOEL 2:23

Everything He does is for our good. Even chronic illness. The worst thing I used to do (and am trying my hardest not to do anymore) is complain, groan, moan, sigh, wince, etc. even when I'm completely by myself. The more I dwelled on it (which is really like saying "living for it") the worse it became.

Now when I catch myself doing any of the aforementioned, I stop as fast as I can and thank God for the good aspect of the illness (yes, there are some) and for what I can do instead of what I can't.

Dear God; Help me consider my Fibromyalgia as part of the rains in my life. In Jesus' name. Amen.

*

August 18th

The Lord is wonderfully good to those who wait for Him and seek Him.

LAMENTATIONS 3:25

Heaven never has a busy signal. There are no passwords to key in. We are free to talk about whatever, whenever. He isn't only there as a "magic genie", but also as Our Father and Brother and Comforter, Our Friend.

Dear God; Patience is the hardest of all virtues. Help me to remember that I'll never get Your voicemail, You don't have Caller ID to turn my away, and I seek Your face, not your back. Amen.

*

August 19th
So he got up and ate and drank and the food gave him enough strength to travel forty days and forty nights to Mount Sinai, the mountain of God.
1 KINGS 19:8

Why is it we are never satisfied with "enough"? Have we ever considered that this is what God intended for us to have? There are a lot of successful "type A personalities" out there, who are names on headstones now because there was no such thing as "enough" in their lives. God's success and the world's are two different things. As for me, my success means to me that I'm happy just searching out my own patches of sunshine.

Dear God; Help us to remember food's intention so we are no longer gluttons. Food is Your simple miracle for us. Let us never lose sight of that. Amen.

*

August 20th
But this is the Lord's reply. I would no more reject my people than I would change My laws of night and day, than earth and sky.
JEREMIAH 33:25

I cannot imagine myself rejecting God under any circumstances. Yet, when I let people wait on me when I am perfectly capable of doing it myself, I reject Him. When I know what the Bible says about "bearing witness" and I tell someone something that is gossip (just this once), or I tell a "little white lie" (no one will know, it won't hurt), I reject Him. My own actions need to come under scrutiny all the time.

Dear God; You can never reject me. Make me so I can never reject You. Amen.

*

August 21st
The eyes of the Lord search the whole earth in order to strengthen those whose hearts are fully committed to Him...

2 CHRONICLES 16:9

That word "fully" is very important, especially in my relationship with Him. Whenever I hear someone say to be committed to the Lord, I stubbornly insist that I already am. Sometimes, however, I can't recall what the sermon was about because I paid more attention to the hideous or out-of-place clothes (by my standards) of the folks around me. I then realize that I have to focus more on the word "fully".

Dear God; Strengthen my heart and commitment to You. In Jesus' name. Amen.

*

August 22nd
Now the vine is growing in the wilderness, where the ground is hard and dry.

EZEKIEL 19:13

I'm not much on gardening. All I know is that hard, dry ground doesn't produce much of anything. I want to produce my very best for Him so I'm going to show up in that wilderness garden with seeds, water, digger, and whatever else I need to be part of the vine's growth.

Dear God; Help me embrace Jesus (the vine) so that I am nothing but receptive. Thank You. Amen.

*

August 23rd
Show your fear of God by standing up in the presence of elderly people and showing respect for the aged. I am the Lord.

LEVITICUS 19:32

In other countries the elderly are revered as treasures to be learned from. Here, in America, they are a burden to be ignored, shunned, ridiculed, and sometimes; abused. He is thousands of years old, yet we respect Him, why not save some for our own elderly?

Dear God; America treats its senior population like something to be discarded and forgotten instead of respecting them. Help me remember to add the countless nursing home residents to my prayer list. Amen.

*

August 24th
Worry weighs a person down; an encouraging word cheers a person up.
PROVERBS 12:25

There are so many verses devoted to our words in the Bible. Sometimes, in the more delicate situations, words get in the way. We are His mouthpieces. We should all remember that every time we open our mouths. It takes seconds to make or break a day, the choice is ours.

Dear God; It is so tempting to pass along “horror stories” to anyone experiencing illness (Fibromyalgia or anything else we know about) but it is just as easy to give someone a pep talk. Help my words build, not destroy. Amen.

*

August 25th
Let no other nation proudly exult into its own prosperity though it will be higher than the clouds, for all are doomed. They will land in the pit along with all the proud people of the world.
EZEKIEL 31:14

When I was in grade school, the expression used for “stuck up” was “acting big”. Whenever I came home from school complaining to my Mother that so-and-so “acts big”, my Mother, not up on the slang of the day, always replied, “she should, she is big.” How do you act big without acting “too big for your britches”? I want to be proud of myself, but not prideful. Is that even possible? I keep a tight reign on my examination of conscience, just in case.

Dear God; Let me exhibit healthy self-confidence without every crossing over into pride. Thank You. Amen.

*

August 26th
So you should realize that just as a parent disciplines a child, the Lord your God disciplines you to help you.

DEUTERNOMY 8:5

If no one ever taught us right from wrong, we would never learn it. The hardest part is self-discipline. Why do we do things we know better than to do? Do we really think He won't notice? Even if we're all by ourselves. If we run a red light on a lonely piece of road and no cop catches us, isn't it still against the law?

Self-discipline is the only area where we can help God out, but we do still have to answer to Him.

Dear God; You correct me because You love me. You want to watch Your children grow. Please correct me so I may grow in You. Amen.

*

August 27th
Do not neglect the spiritual gift you received...

1 TIMOTHY 4:14

Every person has a God-given gift (or talent), even if we aren't sure what He's called us to do with it yet. Any talent is a skill that requires practice. The more we do a thing the better we become at that something. If I hadn't played the piano in thirty years, yet suddenly found myself booked into a concert hall as the main bill, how do you think I would feel? God gives us talents for a reason. I'm going to start to develop them and see where it leads.

Dear God; Let each of us practice his or her gifts. Practice builds skills. Amen.

*

August 28th
Now stand here and see the great thing the Lord is about to do.
1 SAMUEL 12:16

Everything the Lord does is wonderful. Everything. No matter how big or how small. It is so wonderful to be allowed to witness it all from sunrise to sunset. Even the fact that my eyes opened this morning and my feet hit the floor is a great thing that He has done.
All we have to do is say "thank You".

Dear God; I am on the verge of something, and I'm excited to see what You will do. Thank you for counting me in. Amen.

*

August 29th
The cherubim spread their wings out over the Ark, forming a canopy over the carrying poles.
2 CHRONICLES 5:8

If angels take care of poles, don't you think they'll look after us, too? Some people believe that the invisible friends most children have are actually their guardian angels. Children are young and innocent enough to still see the angels even if adults can't. Maybe this is why they are so adamant about their invisible friends being real? At any rate, it is nice to know that angels are here to protect us ever step of the way.

Dear God; Thank You for the angels who surround me and watch over me in all that I do. Amen.

*

August 30th
Be courageous! Let us fight bravely to save our people and the cities of our God. May the Lord's will be done.
1 CHRONICLES 19:13

It takes courage to do His will because He usually asks us to step out of our "comfort zone". This takes every drop of courage we have sometimes as well as real faith. We're always afraid that He'll abandon us half way through or any of a multitude of things will go wrong. God won't ever let us down; He can't, He loves us too much.

Dear God; The nicest part of heeding Your call is that I know that You provide whatever I lack. In Jesus' name. Amen.

*

August 31st
...Spring up, O Well! Yes, sing about it! Sing of this well which princes dug, which great leaders hollowed out with their scepters and staffs.
NUMBERS 21:17-18

People have taken to carrying bottles of water wherever they go. Concession stands in most places now sell bottled water. There is the advice from medical professionals to drink eight glasses of water per day. Jesus tells us we will never thirst if we come to Him. We know how important water is to us, but the Word of God is even more important.

Dear God; Water is the stuff we can't do without. Let us truly sing Your praises for this. Amen.

SEPTEMBER

September 1st
I will praise You forever, O God, for what You have done. I will wait for Your mercies in the presence of Your people.

PSALM 52:9

Praise is there for the whole day. What's wrong with taking the Bible to lunch? Why can't we tell him we love Him anytime of day, all day? Reading the Psalms has to be one of the best pick-me-ups around. We can't praise God and give Him thanks, and stay depressed. It just isn't possible.

Dear God; Let it be my life's goal to wake up every single morning with praise for You on my lips (despite the Fibromyalgia). Amen.

*

September 2nd
So King Solomon became richer and wiser than any other king in all the earth.

1 KINGS 10:23

What if there was a "National count-your-blessings Day"? What would your list look like? How many volumes would it fill? Yes, it is good to be grateful for material things and for the prosperity God has given us, as long as we don't worship them as the world does.

Dear God; Wisdom is like a cleaner for glasses that allow me to clearly see that the riches that I have - the best kind there are - have nothing whatsoever to do with material, monetary things. In Jesus' name. Amen.

*

September 3rd
Asking God, the glorious Father of our Lord Jesus Christ, to give you Spiritual wisdom and understanding, so that you might grown in your knowledge of God.

EPHESIANS 1:17

I am fortunate that I can belong to Bible Study through my church, buy Bible Study materials for individual use, even study the Bible over the internet. When I go into my favorite Christian bookstore, I am always amazed at the number of Christian lifestyle books there are to help us grow in Christ.

Dear God; Every day, I read and study Your Word as well as books about how to live my life as Your servant, all to get to know You better. When I get discouraged, let me realize how far I've come since the day I recited the Sinner's Prayer. Let that knowledge keep me on the right path. Amen.

*

September 4th
From there you will search for the Lord your God. And if you search for Him with all your heart and soul, you will find Him.

DEUTERONOMY 4:29

God isn't hard to find. Look around. There, in the sunrise as it glints off the water, in the dimpled grin of a baby, in the wide eyes of a toddler, in the praying, gnarled hands of the elderly. In our hearts. In the eyes of the beholder.

Dear God; I am indeed searching for You with all I am and all I have. I pray to find You. Amen.

*

September 5th
...People judge by outward appearance, but the Lord looks at a person's thoughts and intentions.

1 SAMUEL 16:7

Wouldn't it be something if we could see others the way God does? There would be no more prejudice, no more hate, and no more wars. There would be nothing but love and kindness. Since we know that God sees the "real" us, why are all those things still here?

Dear God; Let me see through Your eyes. Amen.

*

September 6th
O my God, I have been bold enough to pray this prayer because You have revealed that You will build a house for me - an eternal dynasty!
1 CHRONICLES 17:25

God is preparing a place in heaven for us at this very moment. I've always wondered if He doesn't take something away from the building (like a gemstone or something) when we sin and put it back when we repent. It will be just what each of us needs, and then some. God meets our needs and His blessings never stop pouring down on us - even into eternity.

Dear God; I don't care what my home in Heaven looks like, as long as it handicap accessible! Amen.

*

September 7th
But when his heart and mind were hardened with pride, he was brought down from his royal throne and stripped of his glory.
DANIEL 5:20

In my mind, I'm Superior Woman, but my body always reigns me in. It would be embarrassing to get too big for your britches and have to be brought down to size anyway. Especially if done publicly. I'm grateful to have something in my life that works like a sandbag on a balloon.

Dear God; Thank You for the Fibromyalgia that keeps me humble. Amen.

*

September 8th
Let us find a good musician to play the harp for you whenever the tormenting spirit is bothering you. The harp music will quiet you, and you will be well again.
1 SAMUEL 16:16

Music is my answer for everything. Especially Christian music. When I'm not praying, I'm listening to good music. It really does quiet me and take the frazzle out of my nerves. Pretty soon, I'm singing along and all is well again. It makes the day go faster, too.

Dear God; Help me remember that there are no bad days. Some days are just better than others. When Fibromyalgia begins to torment me, I look through my collection to find good music or a natural relaxation tape to calm me down. In Jesus' name. Amen.

*

September 9th
A good person produces good words from a good heart, and an evil person produces evil words from an evil heart.

MATTHEW 12:35

We can't say what we aren't feeling. Haven't you ever blurted something out that you wish you hadn't? Where did that come from? It's so easy to turn around and snap out a nasty retort when Jesus would rather hear a kind word (and He is listening), or no replay at all. Every time we profess ourselves to be Christian, the world tunes in an ear. Pretty soon our mouths will get the hang of it and we won't even have to profess it anymore.

Dear God; As my eyes are the windows of the my soul, my mouth is the mirror of my heart. Please, Father, help me remember that my words are a witness for Your Word. In Jesus' name. Amen.

*

September 10th
This is the message He has given us to announce to you; God is light and there is no darkness in Him at all.

1 JOHN 1:5

If I would walk into a dark cave, I would be in darkness. If, however, I had a lantern with me, I would have light and not have to worry about stumbling or anything else. Once light is introduced into darkness, there is only light and no more darkness. God's love is the light in an otherwise dark world. If we turn towards His light, we'll never see darkness again.

Dear God; Let there be no darkness in me, either, as I live today for You. Amen.

*

September 11th
In the same way, let your good deeds shine for all to see, so that everyone will praise your heavenly Father.

MATTHEW 5:16

Some people fret because they can't open a homeless shelter or change the world or lay hands on others and heal them. All of those are wonderful, but I like to start small. When I see someone without a smile, I give them one of mine. Simple, common courtesy is easy; Jesus did it all the time.

Dear God; Help my actions proclaim my faith loud and clear, to glorify You. Amen.

*

September 12th
...Strengthen those who have tired hands, and encourage those who have weak knees.

ISAIAH 35:3

Whenever I take pain medication, I pray that it works without side effects. Whenever I go to one of my doctors, I pray that He lets him have the knowledge to know what is best. I go into my exercise classes that same way. All of these things are tools that God uses. Sort of like "a kiss to make it better". I love it when I'm in His arms!

Dear God; You alone have what we need to get on with our lives. Let us come to You for all the things medication doesn't give us. In Jesus' name. Amen.

*

September 13th
He rescues them from the grave so they may live in the light of the living.

JOB 33:30

Every "near death experience" story I have every heard talks about a bright light. The Bible speaks of God as a light and about Jesus as "the light of the world". We are all supposed to be prisms, reflecting His light. We are supposed to be filled with peace and joy - to ourselves "lightly".

Dear God; Even in death, we will see Your Light at the end of the tunnel. May we always follow the Light. Amen.

*

September 14th
Keep away from angry, short-tempered people, or you will learn to be like them and endanger your soul.

PROVERBS 22:24-25

Everyone loses his or her temper sometimes. Unfortunately, there are some people who seem to be professionals at it, devoting their lives to it. Some people are always angry ("stressed", the world calls it, "good excuse", I sarcastically call it) and it makes it hard to be around them. When someone is chronically negative, it becomes old after awhile, and unfortunately, contagious.

I like to live my life on the positive side in hopes that it never gets old and becomes very contagious.

Dear God; Negative, complaining people are a real test of patience. If I must bear them, like sitting by them at school or work, let me keep the climate positive and keep praying to You. Amen.

*

September 15th
The godly eat to their hearts' content, but the belly of the world goes hungry.

PROVERBS 13:25

God wants us to gorge ourselves on His Word. That's why the Bible is as big as it is. That's why you can read the same passage a zillion times and get something different out of it each time. Gluttony in all other areas is sinful, but never in reading the Bible. So what have we got to lose? Except, maybe, Satan.

Dear God; The only place where gluttony does not count is in reading Your Word. Let me eat until I waddle in that aspect. Thank You. Amen.

*

September 16th
...In Jesus we are partners in suffering and in the Kingdom and in patient endurance...

REVELATION 1:9

On my prayer table, I have a little roll-on bottle of pain lotion. That way, I remember to offer my pain up to Jesus. No matter how bad I feel, Jesus felt worse on that cross with the nails and the thorns. All I have to do is look to the crucifix; that sweet, gentle face so tormented. My face will never look like Jesus' did, and for that, I am grateful.

Dear God; Jesus suffered so for me. Thank You for allowing me to suffer my various Fibromyalgia symptoms so I may suffer for You. Amen.

*

September 17th
For You have rescued me from my death; You have kept my feet from slipping. So now I can walk in Your presence, O God, in Your life-giving light.

PSALM 56:13

When we stop dwelling on what we don't have and start being grateful for what we do have, we can find lots of blessings to count. Even if some things don't work as well as others, at least I have them, and I can use the things that do work to help others.

Dear God; Thank You for my legs and my feet. Though they get stiff and achy, they still work. They still fit on Your narrow path. I thank You for my eyes that I may see Your Light. In Jesus' name. Amen.

*

September 18th
Send out Your light and Your truth; let them guide me. Let them lead me to Your holy mountain to the place where You live.

PSALM 43:3

I always want Him to guide me in His truth. It is so easy to get caught up in lies, whether our own (it rarely ends with one lie), or Satan's, or the world's.

Truth takes much less effort than lies. We even teach our children to lie (when the phone rings, "If that's so-and-so, I'm not home.") I'm tired of lies. I don't like being lied to anymore than anyone else does. His truth brings His light, which leads to our salvation.

Dear God; I'm going to let Your light show me the way in an ever-darkening world. Amen.

*

September 19th
...Get to know the God of your ancestors. Worship and serve Him with your whole heart and a willing mind. For the Lord sees every heart and understands and knows every plan and thought. If you seek Him, you will find Him. But if you forsake Him, He will reject you forever.
1 CHRONICLES 28:9

Renewing my mind is the biggest challenge I have ever had to face. I've even had to reorganize the pictures on my wall to refocus myself. But I could never imagine myself backsliding into Atheism or the like. Yes, it is a struggle to lead the sort of life Christ wants me to, but I refuse to entertain any other choice in the matter.

Dear God; Who could ever forsake You? Renew my heart and mind so I will desire only Your will. Amen.

*

September 20th
O my God, be attentive to all the prayers made to You in this place.
2 CHRONICLES 6:40

When I was a kid, I thought that church was the only place to pray. Then, as I grew older, I realized that He listens to our prayers no matter where we are or what we're doing for Him. That's why He's such an awesome God. He loves us so much that His ears are always tuned to our voices.

Dear God; Please listen to my prayers, no matter where I am. Amen.

*

September 21st
But the captain of the guard allowed some of the poorest people to stay behind in Judah to care for the vineyards and fields.

2 KINGS 25:12

The poor have always been treated like garbage. We pat ourselves on the back because we give hand outs, but we turn up our noses when one of "them" gets into trouble with the law, or makes some sort of mistake. They need our love and prayers more than our pity, sneering, or any sort of judgment.

Dear God; Who are the poorest? Financially? Spiritually? It is not up to me to pass judgment. The poorest could be the happiest and isn't that what matters most? Amen.

*

September 22nd
I command you to love each other in the way that I love you.

JOHN 15:12

If we bless others and follow the path of our love walk, we are showing others God and all His majesty. We are sharing Him with others, evangelizing without words. It only takes seconds, yet the possibilities are endless.

Dear God; Let me bless someone today with Your love. In Jesus' name. Amen.

*

September 23rd
I know that You are pleased with me, for You have not let my enemy triumph over me.

PSALM 41:11

I can tell that He is pleased with me. No enemy can ever defeat me. God is rooted firmly in my corner. No matter what malady comes my way, I have it, it never has me. Some days I have to remind myself of that more than others. I am a firm believer in keeping a smile on my face because that smile will dig deep into my heart and mind and soul, if only I let it. Then I am never lost.

Dear God; Yes, I can feel that You are pleased with me. You have seen fit to give me Fibromyalgia, but the pocketful of smiles You also gave me is much more plentiful. Your word and the smile You have given me are all the weaponry I need! Thank you in Jesus' Holy name. Amen.

*

September 24th

In all matters requiring wisdom and balanced judgment, the king found the advice of these young men to be ten times better than that of all the magicians and enchanters in his entire kingdom.

DANIEL 1:20

There are so many books, toys and movies out there aimed at kids that are the occult in thin disguise. The world is a scary enough place without opening kids up to this at such an early age. I want to keep my focus on the Supernatural (the one that counts), so I can help keep kids' focus where it belongs.

Dear God; There is a difference between the Supernatural and the occult. Help me to never forget that and always keep my mind on the right one. Amen.

*

September 25th

They will never again be hungry or thirsty, and they will be fully protected from the scorching noontime heat. For the Lamb who stands in front of the throne will be their Shepherd. He will lead them to the springs of life-giving water. And God will wipe away all their tears.

REVELATION 7:16-17

What a comforting, calming image. His big hand wiping away our tears. I can't wait until I can actually stand face-to-face with Him and wrap my arms around Him. He has given me so much, that my chronic illness is only a little flake of paint off of the masterpiece that is I; that is each of us.

Dear God; I'm glad You are there to help me at all times, but I hope I don't need my tears dried up anytime soon. Amen.

*

September 26th

You will see neither wind nor rain, says the Lord, but this valley will be filled with water. You will have plenty for yourselves and for your cattle and your other animals.

2 KINGS 3:17

In our "more, more, more" society, "plenty" seems to have gotten lost along the way. God gives us enough for each one of us. He knows what our portion should be, not what we want it to be.

If we just listen and obey when He says "enough", we'll learn a whole new lifestyle-the one He wants us to have, and isn't that why we're here in the first place?

Dear God; You always give me "plenty". Help me to not take it for granted, not abuse it in any way. Amen.

*

September 27th

He may have a great army, but they are just men. We have the Lord our God to help us and to fight our battles for us!

2 CHRONICLES 32:8

Just chronic illness. Any problem we could ever think of has the word "just" in front of it because God is behind us. All we have to do is step aside and let God fight all of our battles (before we ourselves have messed everything so badly first).

We need to give all our problems to God before we try to handle them ourselves. God is our "secret weapon", not our last resort.

Dear God; Thank You for being on my side against the uphill battle of Fibromyalgia. Amen.

*

September 28th
But now the Lord my God has given me peace on every side, and I have no enemies and all is well.

1 KINGS 5:4

Positive or negative. Good or bad. Peaceful or anxiety-ridden. We can make the choice of what our day is going to be before we even get out of bed in the morning. It's up to us. I'm convinced that life is our attitude towards it. Life is too short to make the wrong decision - even for a day.

Dear God; Peace. The perfect gift. Life is what we make it. Help me realize that as I embrace Your Peace. Amen.

*

September 29th
As for me, I look to the Lord for His help. I wait confidently for God to save me, and my God will certainly help me.

MICAH 7:7

Isn't it great to know that there is one four-letter word God listens for? In fact, it's music to His ears. Help! It's just that simple. When we're feeling the first tingling of an attack by Satan, or we're shoulder-deep in trouble, that simple little word becomes a powerful, big prayer. When put to the test, it really does work.

Dear God; Let me remember that one of the most powerful words in the English language is "Help!" Amen.

*

September 30th
But Peter and the apostles replied, "We must obey God rather than human authority."

ACTS 5:29

Human beings are social beasts and because of it we often seek each other's opinions. This only gets us in deeper and deeper trouble. We all know to Whom we are to turn.

We just don't want to hear His answer sometimes because obedience can be tough. (Just like any parent/child relationship.) We need to know where our focus belongs and keep it there.

Dear God; Help me say the same as Peter did to all temptation. Amen.

OCTOBER

October 1st
The grass withers, and the flowers fade, but the word of our God stands forever.

ISAIAH 40:8

God's Word stands the test of time. Everything and everyone except God fade away. That's why the only place to put out trust is in God and the Word because they never fade or tarnish. They're always there. Isn't that good to know in the world that changes too fast?

Dear God; As I bury Your Word in my heart, I know that it will never be proven false, and that it will be there no matter when I need it. Amen.

*

October 2nd
Arise, Jerusalem! Let your light shine for all the nations to see! For the glory of the Lord is shining upon you.

ISAIAH 60:1

Each one of us is standing in His spotlight. Each one of us is a shining star. Like auditioning for a show, we each have a talent. What we do with that talent is up to each one of us. When we follow His will for us, we can't help but shine in His glory.

Dear God; Let us bask in the glow of Your glory always! Amen.

*

October 3rd
For You are my hiding place; You protect me from trouble. You surround me with songs of victory.

PSALM 32:7

Christian music is wonderful. Since David wrote the Psalms, we've been singing love songs to Him. Even some secular songs can be lifted up to Him.

If we listen very closely, we can hear Him singing back to us. Crickets in summer, the laughter of children, the crisp Fall wind, even a soft gentle heartbeat. It's endless. Just listen with your heart: that's God singing to you. Isn't it beautiful?

Dear God; Let me remember that I always have You to run to, no matter what. Amen.

*

October 4th
They attacked me at a moment when I was weakest, but the Lord upheld me.
2 SAMUEL 22:19

Our bodies attack us sometimes. They can be both friend and foe. God gives us such maladies to draw us closer to Him, to let us rely on Him to the fullest. God holds us up, or at least holds our hands. We have an advantage over the rest because we know God's nurturing side on a first-hand basis, and we can even feel His embrace if we just quiet ourselves.

Dear God; You support me when Fibromyalgia makes me weak and/or miserable, or at least tries to. Fibromyalgia brings me closer to You, so thank You. Amen.

*

October 5th
Be silent, and know that I am God!...
PSALM 46:10

When we choose to be positive, we choose to hear from God. It's easier to reach a happy heart than a hardened one. If we keep ourselves open to Him, we'll hear from Him. If we don't know His voice or His ways, how can we recognize Him?

Dear God; When I complain that I never hear from You, remind me to shut up and listen! In Jesus' name. Amen.

*

October 6th
But they will become his subjects, so that they can learn how much better it is to serve Me than to serve earthly rules.

2 CHRONICLES 12:8

We fall into the trap of worshipping the things of this world, including the people, when our focus belongs on the Kingdom above. No idol here on earth can catapult us to heaven, no matter how much we bow to it. Serving God is why we're here. Satan makes other things seem more inviting, but they are all his lies. I want to serve only the truth.

Dear God; Earthly rulers are money, latest fashion fads, etc. Help me keep my face turned only toward You. Amen.

*

October 7th
Yet I will rejoice in the Lord! I will be joyful in the God of my salvation.

HABAKKUK 3:18

Once, several years ago, a visiting sales manager at the company that I worked for spent a couple of days in the department I worked in at the time. Negativism ran rampant throughout the entire office. This man observed me, in the midst of all that, and despite my illness, calm and happy. When he finally asked me about it, I told him that I was so busy rejoicing in my Savior that my heart didn't have time for anything else.

Dear God; I want to get to the point that the first thing I do every morning, as soon as my eyes open, is to rejoice in You! Amen.

*

October 8th
For my yoke fits perfectly, and the burden I give you is light.

MATTHEW 11:30

At my last trip to the grocery store, I noticed that everything today is "light" (or "lite"). That seems to sell better than the rest. If we're eating "light" foods, why do we all seem to be anything but "light"? We growl like hungry lions. We rush from place to place of our own choosing. Our modern devices do everything faster, yet we have less time for each other, and no time for God. "Light " might be big in grocery stores, but the rest of our lives seem to be anything but. Maybe we need to take the time to "light"-en up?

Dear God; Help me remember that there are those who are in worse straits than I am, and help me remember to give You praise! Amen.

*

October 9th

I have loved you even as the Father has loved Me. Remain in My love.

JOHN 15:9

I cannot imagine being anywhere but in His love. Where else should I go? No alternative even begins to look appealing. No matter where I would go, God's love is always there. I can't run from it (even if I ever wanted to), or hide from it. He loves me with that strong of a love. Doesn't it feel great?

Dear God; I am blessed to be in Your love. What could ever entice me away from You? Nothing or no one even comes close. Amen.

*

October 10th

The Lord's promises are pure, like silver refined in a furnace, purified seven times over.

PSALM 12:6

Sometimes fire can be a good thing. God's heat purifies His promises. He can't lie, He's God! God never breaks a promise. As His child, I try to keep my promises and not make promises that I can't keep. All of God's promises in the Bible came true, even those that took years and years. With a little patience, they'll come true for me, too.

Dear God; You have never broken a promise. It is not in Your nature. Help me not break any promises either, so I may display Your nature. Thank You. Amen.

*

October 11th
For my sake, O Lord, and according to Your will, You have done all these great things and have them made known.

1 CHRONICLES 17:19

Everything He does is great. He can't do anything small or insignificant, it isn't in His nature. The people that He chooses to work through may remain nameless and faceless, but they accomplish His tasks. Technology and all good things are escalating by leaps, and He is behind every one of them.

Dear God; I am reminded of the great strides in medicine in the 20th century alone. Every day, You let us know about something else soon to be available. You give Fibromyalgia patients hope. Amen.

*

October 12th
I wait quietly before God, for my hope is in Him.

PSALM 62:5

Hope. One of the most precious treasures known to mankind. Above and beyond gems and cash is hope. Without it, what would we have? There is no such thing as "hopelessness", not as long as we can still look up and pray.

Dear God; Sometimes it's good to sit in silence (You know the tribulations we bring before You, You have heard them often enough) and just envision God on His throne. Help me to take some time to do that. Amen.

*

October 13th
He will give you all you need, from day to day, if you make the Kingdom of God your primary concern.

LUKE 12:31

In and of ourselves, we can do nothing. He gives us all we have and are. So why then would our focus be anywhere else? We can't do anything without seeing God in all our surroundings, in all people, all we have to do is look.

Dear God; You are my priority. Please give me a Kingdom-mind. Amen.

October 14th
So you see, God is with us. He is our leader. His priests blow their trumpets and lead us into battle against you. O people of Israel, do not fight against the Lord, the God of your ancestors, for you will not succeed.
2 CHRONICLES 13:12

God leads us into and out of each day. Sometimes willingly, sometimes kicking and screaming, but He always leads us. God is always with us in every circumstance we face, good or not so good. All we have to do is acknowledge Him, talk to Him, listen to Him, and obey Him.

Dear God; Help me to always go with You, not against You, in all I do. Thank You. Amen.

*

October 15th
And may these words that I have prayed in the presence of the Lord be before Him constantly, day and night, so that the Lord our God may uphold my cause and the cause of His people Israel, fulfilling our daily needs.
1 KINGS 8:59

Trusting God so completely that He fulfills our needs every day, all day, is easier said than done sometimes. He fulfills "needs" not "wants". God isn't a genie, but He does require our trust and submission. An ongoing dialogue with Him all day is actually, I believe, what is really center in all of our lives.

Dear God; Help me realize that You will meet every need, so I can go on carefree! Amen.

*

October 16th
...Plant the good seeds of righteousness, and you will have a crop of My love. Plow up the hard ground of your hearts, for now is the time to seek the Lord, that He may come and shower righteousness upon you.
HOSEA 10:12

A shower of righteousness (especially for the whole world) sounds great. Acceptance sounds even better.

God pours His blessings out on us, but it's up to us to gather them up. It's up to us to accept them. The "hard ground of our hearts" can only win out if we allow it to.

Dear God; As I seek You, let me accept the righteousness You will pour on me so I can walk in it. Amen.

*

October 17th
And the Lord spoke kind and comforting words to the angel who talked with me.

ZECHARIAH 1:13

Angels don't always come to us wearing halos and wings. They come in all sorts of forms and sizes. God uses any means He can to get to us. We just have to keep our ears and hearts open.

Dear God; Open my ears so I may hear Your words come out of any and all "angels" You choose to use. Amen.

*

October 18th
You are my strength; I wait for You to rescue me, for You, O God, are my place of safety.

PSALM 59:9

When I was a kid, I played games that had "safety zones" in them. Now, as an adult, I realize that I've always had a "safety zone", and all I have to do to reach it is pray. Isn't it wonderful to know that we are safe in His arms no matter what?

Dear God; No matter how bad the Fibromyalgia gets (or how badly the medications fail) I am at peace because I know that You are a safe haven. Amen.

*

October 19th

The Lord Almighty says, "The day of judgment is coming, burning like a furnace. The arrogant and wicked will be burned up like straw on that day. They will be consumed like a tree -- roots and all."

MALACHI 4:1

God has a judgment all picked out for each of us. I just have to remember that it isn't the day in the mall when the clothes offend me. It isn't when I hear a string of four-letter words from a ten-year-old, or when I'm at a picnic where the alcohol is flowing like a river, or when I judge anyone for anything. It's the day of His choosing, not mine.

Dear God; Let me remember that You are the One doing the judging, and You do not require my input. Amen.

*

October 20th

These people honor me with their lips, but their hearts are far away.

MATTHEW 15:8

How many of us use Christian or Charismatic catch phrases but are just speaking into the wind? Our hearts just aren't where they are supposed to be. Do we really believe what we're saying or is it just a lot of words that sound good? Does our behavior reflect our words or is it "do-as-I-say-and-not-as-I-do" time? Our mouths are a wonderful tool when used correctly, when our words come from a right heart.

Dear God; Let what comes out of my lips come from my heart. Amen.

*

October 21st

Jesus replied, "Let those who are spiritually dead care for their own dead. Your duty is to go and preach the coming of the Kingdom of God."

LUKE 9:60

Not all of us are called to be preachers, teachers, or evangelists, so how do we get the Word of God out? By our example. If we follow the example of Jesus, we should have no problem in passing it on. Even (maybe especially) when no one is looking, are we still Christ-like? The world scrutinizes Christians more closely. Give them something to watch!

Dear God; Let me be alive in You. Amen.

*

October 22nd
If you are filled with light, with no dark corners, then your whole life will be radiant, as though a floodlight is shining on you.

LUKE 11:36

We have to be careful of those dark corners. We all have them; fear or anxiety, or doubt, or self-pity. Whatever we choose to call them, they are there. Prayer brings the Light to us, even those dark, cobweb corners, if we just ask.

Dear God; Be my flashlight for all those dark corners. Amen.

*

October 23rd
His anger lasts for a moment, but His favor lasts a lifetime! Weeping may go on all night, but joy comes in the morning.

PSALM 30:5

Nighttime has always been my time to talk to God (if I don't fall asleep in mid-sentence). I ask forgiveness, guidance, and offer Thanksgiving. God is always there to meet me. He never fails to show up. Things always look bleak at night, but I know that when the sun comes up, He has blessed me with another day, another chance.

Dear God; Show me how to be slow to anger. Show me how to pass Your love on. All I want is Your favor. Thank You in Your Son's name. Amen.

*

October 24th
Life itself was in Him, and this life gives light to everyone.

JOHN 1:4

Some people are described as being "full of life". Everyone who is alive has life in them. Some just embrace life better than others. Others just seem to survive, to vegetate. Bouncy, bubbly, upbeat people are the best kind to be around. They can't help but be Christians.

Dear God; I gladly take the lantern from You, Jesus. I want Your path to be illuminated so well that I can't possibly stumble. Amen.

*

October 25th
...Be strong and courageous, and do the work. Don't be afraid or discouraged by the size of the task, for the Lord God, my God, is with you. He will not fail you or forsake you. He will see to it that all the work related to the Temple of the Lord is finished correctly.

1 CHRONICLES 28:20

Sometimes my "to do list" seems as big as the stone tablets that Moses received when he went up the mountain. It weighs as heavily on me, too. It has always driven me nuts to have something hanging over my head. When I was still able to hold down a forty-hour-a-week job, it got harder and harder for me to have the time and/or stamina to do things, so I let a lot of things slide.

Now that I have more time in my day, I'm learning to pace myself. The mess will still be there after my nap. It's still hard not to overdo, but I know the consequences, so I ask Him to slow me down. Talking to Him always does wonders for me.

Dear God; We Fibromyalgia patients have to adhere to the word "pacing". You provide the task, but if we just take in "bite-sized" pieces, You will give us what we need to cross it off our "to do" list. Amen.

*

October 26th
I have given you an example to follow. Do as I have done to you.

JOHN 13:15

Jesus is our example. Some people say we aren't ever going to be perfect anyway, so why bother? Many times, we're the only bit of Jesus others are submitted to at all. How can we lead them into the flock if our behavior is worse than theirs? Focus on the love walk and all else will fall into place.

Dear God; W.W.J.D. is more than a fashion fad. Help me ask it in all that I do. Amen.

*

October 27th
I am leaving you with a gift- peace of mind and heart. And the peace I give isn't like the peace the world gives.

JOHN 14:27

When I think of Jesus' peace, the first thing that comes to mind is "tranquility". A lazy leaf swirling into a gentle stream, riding on the silent, sun-glistened water is tranquil. That's the kind of peace Jesus wants us to have. Wherever the current leads is God's will for us. We are in His hands.

Dear God; Let me embrace Your peace forever. Amen.

*

October 28th
The Lord is my light and my salvation-so why should I be afraid? The Lord protects me from danger- so why should I tremble?

PSALM 27:1

Isn't it good to know that God is our protector? We need never be afraid of anything or anyone. No one on this earth or under this earth can come against us. Just go to God. No questions asked. He will soothe it all away.

Dear God; It is not easy to be afraid in the light of day especially when the Light is from You. Help me keep this in my heart. Thank You. Amen.

*

October 29th
Do not despise these small beginnings, for the Lord rejoices to see the work begin...

ZECHARIAH 4:10

No matter how tiny that first step, how insignificant to the whole finished project, we have to start somewhere. No matter how good the idea, if it never leaves the mind (for whatever reason), it isn't ever going to see reality. He knows that a project (or even a simple task like brushing teeth) is a series of steps. The first step has to be taken so the last one can come. He's there to encourage us all along the way.

Dear God; A ski-slope begins with a snowflake. Let me be proud to be a snowflake. Amen.

*

October 30th
Keep alert and pray. Otherwise temptation will overpower you. For though the spirit is willing enough, the body is weak!

MATTHEW 26:41

At the first nibbling of Satan at my soul, I run to God as fast as I can. We like to limp along and convince ourselves that it isn't Satan after all, that God wants us to go a new way. If we limp along enough, Satan will pounce and we'll be in sin so deep God has to throw a life-preserver to reach us and reel us in. Wouldn't it just be easier to go to God in the first place?

Dear God; Don't let my weak body get in the way of a strong Spirit. In Jesus' name. Amen.

*

October 31st
Have mercy on me, O God, have mercy! I look to You for protection. I will hide beneath the shadow of Your wings until this violent storm passes.

PSALM 57:1

All storms pass, no matter how violent. Watch for the rainbow afterwards. It always comes, sooner or later. All we have to do is look up. Jesus is the protection we need to fly like eagles beneath God as He shows us the way. Remember: Eagles always fly close to the Son.

Dear God; Please let this "storm" pass quickly. In the meantime, help me remember that Your feathers never get ruffled. In Jesus' name. Amen.

NOVEMBER

November 1st

Give me wisdom and knowledge to rule them properly for who is able to govern this great nation of yours?

2 CHRONICLES 1:10

We have the privilege - and with any privilege comes responsibility - of choosing the leadership of our government. There is so much hype to cut through to know which way to vote that it becomes challenging. He has the answers we need to go do our duty.

Dear God; Before I go into the voting booth, I'll listen carefully to You, and together we can take back America for You. Amen.

*

November 2nd

I said to myself, "Come now, let's give pleasure a try. Let's look for the good things in life"...

ECCLESIASTES 2:1

Looking for the good in life - in everyone and everything-is a fun game. Some people and things need a lot more scrutiny than others to find it. All in all, pleasure seeking (of the moral kind) is great fun. Everything has good in it, all we have to do is find it.

Dear God; Point out the simple pleasures You have in store for us. For this very moment, though, counting our blessings is just one way to have fun! Thank You. Amen.

*

November 3rd

At least I can take comfort in this; despite the pain, I have not denied the words of the Holy One.

JOB 6:10

I firmly believe that those of us with chronic illness and/ or chronic pain are blessed because we are closer to Him. He knows our special needs and fulfills them. I also believe that we have His ear more readily. What the world deems as a handicap, Heaven sees as a special uniqueness from the heart and hand of God.

Dear God; Despite our Fibromyalgia, we are still Your children. We can make You our priority and live to please You. In Jesus' name. Amen.

*

November 4th
You are not defiled by what you eat, you are defiled by what you say and do.
MATTHEW 15:11

Jesus knew, all those centuries ago, that thoughts, speech, and deed, could make or break us as Christians. In Jesus' day, there weren't nearly as many opportunities to get into trouble as there are today. With Jesus' words in mind, we need to live our lives like He wants of us.

Dear God; Help my feet and tongue bring You joy. Amen.

*

November 5th
Then Jesus was filled with the joy of the Holy Spirit and said, "O Father, Lord of heaven and earth, thank You for hiding the truth from those who think themselves clever, and for revealing it to the childlike. Yes, Father, it pleased You to do it this way."
LUKE 10:21

There is a difference between childish and childlike. Ask anyone who has ever seen a wide-eyed toddler explore his or her world. That's the kind of Christian God wants us to be. He wants the kind like Abram, who didn't question when asked to offer his only son on the altar. He wants the ones like Shadarach, Meshach, and Abednego, who never forsake Him, no matter the consequences.

Maybe that's why Jesus came as a baby, to be our example to never lose that kind of faith.

Dear God; Let the child in me get through this crazy adult world. Amen.

*

November 6th
...You are from below; I am from above. You are of this world; I am not.
JOHN 8:23

Just because I'm "of the world" does not mean that I have to be "worldly". The gravitational pull on Christians is made worse by the pull of Satan. We must know Who we belong to, where our true home is, and act accordingly.

Dear God; When this world gets to be too much, I am glad I can come to You. Amen.

*

November 7th
No longer will you need the sun or moon to give you light, for the Lord your God will be your everlasting light, and He will be your glory.
ISAIAH 60:19

The Light is always with us, even when our minds implore darkness. When our first perceptions of an occurrence are bleak and grim, along He comes with a blazing lantern to let us know everything is going to be all right beyond all possible dreams. The best part of it is, we won't become "battery poor". For a recharge, just pray.

Dear God; You make the Son shine in our hearts! Thank You. Amen.

*

November 8th
You are my refuge and my shield; Your word is my only source of hope.
PSALM 119:114

What other source of hope is there? I don't know how people who don't know God make it through a day. God is rock solid and the most indestructible shield imaginable. He wrote His Word for us. It never changes, even getting stronger and timelier with each passing generation.

Dear God; With Bible in hand, I am unconquerable. Even with it closed beside me, I find comfort.
Thank You. Amen.

*

November 9th
I will certainly give you the wisdom and knowledge you requested. And I will also give you riches, wealth and honor such as no other king has ever had before or will ever have again.

2 CHRONICLES 1:12

Wisdom and understanding are the Bible's top priorities. Everything else is sort of an afterthought. Those are to be our priorities as well. All the "stuff" we hold so dear, God tells us, belongs on the back burner. He gives us ample time in hopes that we give some back to Him everyday.

Dear God; Help me to remember that You are God, not a genie. Help my requests be for the things that aren't material in life. Thank You. Amen.

*

November 10th
My eyes are red with weeping; darkness covers my eyes. My friends scorn me, but I pour out my tears to God.

JOB 16:16,20

Everyone agrees that the best kind of tears are tears of joy. Whatever kind of tears flow-frustration, pain, loss, etc.-are always followed by prayer. Joyful tears bring prayers of thanksgiving, and all the others are followed by prayers seeking comfort. He cries right along with us, all the while He dries our tears. He alone has our future in clear sight.

Dear God; I know sometimes it is hard for people who do not have to deal with chronic illness to deal with me and the necessary changes Fibromyalgia has brought and will bring. If my friends desert me, they were not my friends in the first place. Help me to realize this and not cry out in self-pity. Amen.

*

November 11th
God sent John the Baptist to tell everyone about the Light so that everyone might believe because of his testimony.

JOHN 1:7

Would our own personal testimonies turn anyone to Jesus? I'd be willing to carry a pocket-sized flashlight if it leads someone to Jesus' searchlights. I want to be like a toy that glows in the dark, soaking up light in as many ways as possible so I can glow in someone else's darkness.

Dear God; Let me see Jesus' Light all day long. In Jesus' name. Amen.

*

November 12th
The nations of the earth will walk in its light, and the rulers of the world will come and bring their glory to it.

REVELATION 21:24

Wouldn't it be wonderful to have world peace? Not because there are armies standing guard, either. It would be wonderful if the Light would bring love enough to fill every heart in the world to overflowing. It all starts with our own love walk.

Dear God; I pray, Lord, for world leaders that they all walk in the Light that we might follow their example. Amen.

*

November 13th
The Lord Almighty is here among us; the God of Israel is our fortress.

PSALM 46:7

Because I still find Him and His agape so awesome, the knowledge that He is always with me and in me is something I confess to forgetting sometimes. What a great protector and provider who is actually part of us (or are we part of Him?), with us always, Who will never forsake us.

Dear God; Wherever we are, You are there with us, clearing and smoothing the way for us. Let me walk on that path and not stray. Amen and Amen.

November 14th
Surely Your goodness and unfailing love will pursue me all the days of my life and I will live in the house of the Lord forever.
PSALM 23:6

It's really something to realize that He loves us so much that He pursues us every single day of our lives. I love to try to imagine what Heaven will be like, and no matter what I can dream up, I'm sure I'm not doing it justice.

Dear God; As You pursue me, I pursue You. It is an honor to be invited to visit Your house, but to live there is the highest privilege I can imagine. Thank You. Amen.

*

November 15th
Happy is the person who finds wisdom and gains understanding.
PROVERBS 3:13

Wisdom doesn't mean book knowledge, it means Book Knowledge. The more we study the Bible, the more we "understand" (although God is beyond human understanding). When we go into Bible study (formal or on our own) with the right motives, we come out winners.

Dear God; Wisdom and understanding are always mentioned in the same breath in the Bible. These are Your gifts to us. Like any skills, if I don't practice them, I'm not going to have them at all. Help me be very happy today and always. Amen.

*

November 16th
Don't talk too much, for it fosters sin. Be sensible and turn off the flow!
PROVERBS 10:19

I wish I had a loud inner voice that tells me to "shut up" (or maybe it is loud and I'm talking too much to hear it). Have you ever heard your own voice, and thought, "that's me saying that?" Worse yet, have you ever heard your own voice and have no idea how to turn it off? That's when bringing this verse to mind can be a sin-saver.

Dear God; Gossip and judgmental talk (and thoughts) are sin. Help me to know when to shut up! Amen.

*

November 17th
Then his body will become as healthy as a child's, firm and youthful again.
JOB 33:25

Life here on earth isn't half bad. It's actually pretty much fun. When I get to Heaven, I'm promised a new life complete with new body. Bodies in Heaven are perfect. There is no way to get one with any sort of defect. What freedom that promises!

Dear God; In Heaven, there is no Fibromyalgia, or any other illness. There are no angels with broken wings. Help me hang on to this thought when a "pity party" starts to arise. Amen.

*

November 18th
Always be full of joy in the Lord. I say it again - rejoice.
PHILIPPIANS 4:4

Keep your joy. Satan wants to steal it, but I for one, refuse to allow it. I'm too busy using it to give it up. Joy can be found in mundane things and in places we wouldn't give a second thought to. It's so easy to smile or even laugh. If something will be looked back on one day with laughter, why isn't it funny now? A joyless life is no life at all.

Dear God; I cannot think of a better reason to be happy than for happiness' sake. Amen.

*

November 19th
Then they entered into a covenant to seek the Lord, the God of their ancestors, with all their heart and soul. They shouted out their loyalty to the Lord with trumpets blaring and horns sounding.
2 CHRONICLES 15:12,14

This is what Charismatic Contemporary Christian music is all about. We're laying open our hearts to God. Some say it's just rock and roll with Christian lyrics, but countless souls have been won because of it. When our joy bubbles over, I say do whatever you can to get it out.

Dear God; I will shout my praises to You in all I do. Amen.

*

November 20th
The Lord is my strength, my shield from every danger. I trust in Him with all my heart. He helps me, and my heart is filled with joy. I burst out in songs of Thanksgiving.

PSALM 28:7

Thanksgiving is my favorite holiday. It's the only one that commercialism hasn't ruined. It's the day for counting our blessings. Atop that list I always put Jesus. Without Him, there is nothing. We Christians don't know how good we've got it.

Dear God; Thanksgiving is something that we can celebrate all year. Counting our blessings is on going because they are on going. Help me to start a list and watch how fast it grows. Amen and Amen.

*

November 21st
...He lighted the way before me and I walked safely through the darkness.

JOB 29:3

It feels like Jesus has me by the hand, a lantern in His other hand as we sidle along the narrow path in some obscure cave. No matter where He leads us, we can follow without fear. We can trust without hesitation. Christ came to save our lives. All we have to do is let Him.

Dear God; You are my Flashlight after the storm. Amen.

*

November 22nd
He is a light to reveal God to the nations, and He is the glory of your people Israel.

Luke 2:32

If we are to follow the example set by Jesus, we are able to be "a light to reveal God to the nations". We don't need a pulpit or a ministry. All we need is our own lives led in such a way that no one can help but see God everywhere we go and in every situation, and that's what being a Christian is all about.

Dear God; Let my example reveal You to the world. Thank You. Amen.

*

November 23rd
Day after day more men joined David until he had a great army, like the army of God.

1 CHRONICLES 12:22

I can just imagine people, one by one, lining up behind David in an act of trust. Maybe an act of defiance. David, like the rest of us, had God on his side, and he, like the rest of us, was on God's side. What an unbeatable team!

Dear God; We are all part of Your army. So here I am, reporting for duty. Whatever You tell me, I will do. Amen.

*

November 24th
Rise during the night and cry out. Pour out your hearts like water to the Lord. Lift up your hands to him in prayer...

LAMENTATIONS 2:19

All the hands waving the air as the music plays reminds me of a field of flowers. All the heads of the flowers turn toward the sun, while all of us turn toward the Son. Just like the flowers and the sun, we just can't help ourselves, our hands go up to Him.

Dear God; Let me use the nighttime when Fibromyalgia makes me the craziest, to spend with You. In Jesus' name. Amen.

*

November 25th
You chart the path ahead of me and tell me where to stop and rest. Every moment You know where I am.

PSALM 139:3

Whenever I feel lost I know that He will find me. He is always there, all knowing, all loving. He made the path that I walk and He tells me how and when to walk it.

All I have to do is put one foot in front of the other.

Dear God; There is so much security in knowing You. No matter what, You are always there to find me and to be my Navigator and Companion. Amen.

*

November 26th
...Let the smile of Your face shine on us, O Lord.

PSALM 4:6

Isn't it a great way to think of Him, smiling down on us? His smiling face aglow shows us His love for us. Just like any proud parent. We can see His smile in the sunshine, a beautiful sunset, even in the way crisp November air kisses faces on a clear day. His love and approval are all around us, it's our turn to give back.

Dear God; Although the Bible does not record the fact that You ever smiled, Jesus, I know in my heart that you had to, because our Father did. Lord, let me aspire to make You smile. Amen.

*

November 27th
Let everyone see that you are considerate in all you do. Remember, the Lord is coming soon.

PHILIPPIANS 4:5

Manners- a simple "thank you" or holding a door for someone- is a lost part of our culture as a whole. It's up to me to keep manners off the endangered species list. It only takes a moment to walk in love. Every word that comes out of our mouths, every good deed we do can make someone's day. That should make my own day as well.

Dear God; Let me be ready in all I do. Amen.

*

November 28th
Yet I still belong to You; You are holding my right hand.

PSALM 73:23

I remember how good and safe it felt as a little girl when I held the hand of my earthly father, skipping happily beside him, pigtails flapping. When I read this verse, that memory comes to the forefront again. How much better this is that God has me by the hand! Even though I no longer have pigtails that flap, and I can no longer skip, I can still feel good because I belong to Him.

Dear God; Sometimes I'm not sure who is holding onto whom. If You hold my hand, I'll hold Yours. I'll even squeeze it now and again just for so. Amen

*

November 29th
The advice of the wise is like a life-giving fountain; those who accept it avoid the snares of death.

PROVERBS 13:14

Sometimes God uses others as His mouthpieces. It's up to us to listen and obey. A fountain's water is re-circulating. Going around and around, the water looks majestic, but it serves no other purpose; not to drink anyway. We all have to drink in the words of the godly so they don't just go around and around, sounding wonderful, but serving no purpose.

Dear God; Let me accept any and all advice deemed for my good so I can work toward saving my life. Amen.

November 30th

Getting wisdom is the most important thing you can do! And whatever else you do, get good judgment.

PROVERBS 4:7

As I have often confessed to you, I struggle with being judgmental. The type of judgment I strive for is good judgment. I want my judgments to be as positive as the other aspects of my life. Wisdom and good judgment are a natural duo.

Dear God; Good judgment sounds like a contradiction in terms because when someone is "judgmental" he or she uses no wisdom, only emotion, for a negative outcome. Help all my judgments be good ones, Lord. Thank you. Amen

DECEMBER

December 1st
The one who is the true Light, who gives Light to everyone, was going to come into the world.

JOHN 1:9

How do we prepare ourselves for this wonderful season's true meaning? All the rushing around and craziness can take our minds off of the greatest miracle of all. We need to catch our breath and reflect on the Baby who changed the world - and our hearts.

Dear God; Let us remember throughout this most Blessed Season, just what we're celebrating. In Jesus' mighty name. Amen.

*

December 2nd
But I will keep on hoping for You to help me; I will praise You more and more.

PSALM 71:14

The more I know Him, the easier it is to praise Him. The hard part is to stop praising Him. It's a good thing I never have to. I see God in more places than I thought possible. I praise Him more than I ever thought possible. It is so much fun to live this way, how did I ever live any other way?

Dear God; Blessed be Your Holy Name! As long as I am alive, I have hope to be well. I praise You all day long, Lord, because I know that there is no Fibromyalgia in Heaven! Thank You! Amen.

*

December 3rd
There the child [Jesus} grew up healthy and strong. He was filled with wisdom beyond His years, and God placed His special favor upon Him.

LUKE 2:40

Although the Bible doesn't record it, I believe that Jesus grew up in a happy home. He was strong, both physically and mentally. He was God, yet He was a typical little boy growing towards His three years of ministry. God prepared Him well for that.

Dear God; No matter the status of our health, we are special to You. Help me to remember that about myself and everyone. In Jesus' name. Amen.

*

December 4th

So the Lord gave great wisdom to Solomon just as He had promised. And Hiram and Solomon made a formal alliance of peace.

1 KINGS 5:12

Solomon was the wisest man who ever lived. God came through for him more than He promised, just like He will do for us. God loves us so much that He wants to surprise us not just with good, but by giving us His very, very best. The results are usually far beyond our expectations, our wildest dreams.

Dear God; I may not have the "wisdom of Solomon", but I can take what I do have and make my own "alliance of peace" an example to this crazy world. Bless me with the courage that true wisdom brings. Amen.

*

December 5th

Charm is deceptive, and beauty does not last, but a woman who fears the Lord will be greatly praised.

PSALM 31:30

Man or woman, everyone who fears the Lord should be praised. It's easier said than done to trust in God without batting an eye (or dabbing one, anyway). It's easy to say "thy will be done" until a crisis comes along to upset the apple cart. No matter what we have, the ability to give it to God is the best gift of all.

Dear God; Charm and beauty will get me nowhere. Help me to be truly Yours. Amen.

December 6th
The eyes of the Lord search the whole earth in order to strengthen those whose hearts are fully committed to Him...

2 CHRONICLES 16:9

I can't wait until the day I can look into God's eyes. I wonder what color they will be: blue, green, hazel, brown, black, or some color not yet thought of by us humans? If they can see the whole earth and even into the heart, what must they be like? Are they really that big or does He scan something like a huge internet? Only time will tell, but I, for one, am glad He can see me and my heart.

Dear God; Whether my faith or my body needs strength this day, I always know the source of that strength. Thank You. Amen.

*

December 7th
...Fix your thoughts on what is true and honorable and right. Think about things that are pure and lovely and admirable. Think about things that are worthy of praise.

PHILIPPIANS 4:8

This is a shopping list for our thought life. I am just beginning to learn to use it well. It is difficult, for me, anyway, to stop a thought from becoming words (if the thought even registers before the words come). Until this verse wraps itself around my heart and soul, I have copies all over the place.

Dear God; Let these thoughts be the only ones to register with me. Amen.

*

December 8th
Jesus said, "Your problem is you don't know the Scriptures, and you don't know the power of God."

MATTHEW 12:24

There is power in love. That bond is as strong as steel. And that's just "human" love. Imagine what agape is like. Our minds can't comprehend that power, that strength. It is there. We just have to be quiet and bask in it.

Dear God; As I read Your Word, let my mind be a sponge, not a sieve. Thank You. Amen.

*

December 9th
If a tree is cut down, there is hope that it will sprout again and grow new branches.

JOB 14:7

There have been times when I have heard the ominous shout of "timber" in my life. After watching my new pet parakeet meticulously climb (beak and feet), back up from his cage's bottom to his favorite perch, I realize that this is the way we all have to treat our adversity.

Take a deep breath and start climbing, not matter how long it takes or how much of a struggle.

Dear God; Although Fibromyalgia has cut me down, it is not going to keep me down. Please let me bring forth new sprouts and new branches in my life. Amen.

*

December 10th
When He woke up, He rebuked the wind and said to the water, "Quiet down!" Suddenly, the wind stopped and there was a great calm.

MARK 4:39

The very thought of my problems upset me to tears. When I finally did give it to Him, I remembered this verse because such a calm came over me that I only wish I could have given it to God right away.

Dear God; When I need a "great calm", I know where to come. Amen.

*

December 11th
Answer me when I call, O God who declares me innocent. Take away my distress. Have mercy on me and hear my prayer.

PSALM 4:1

Jesus died so we could all be declared innocent. He always hears our prayer. No matter what the distress is, He takes it away and leaves in its place His perfect peace, the gift He was born to give us.

Dear God; Please help me to be distress-free. In Jesus' name. Amen.

*

December 12th

But those who exalt themselves will be humbled and those who humble themselves will be exalted.

MATTHEW 23:12

In this world where winning is everything, emphasis is placed on success so highly that heart attacks are the norm, and the loudest voice gets the floor, being humble is not part of the picture anymore.

Here it is in black and white that some people are going to be "taken down a peg". Since that can mean fire at the bottom of that peg, I, for one, am trying to be humble.

Dear God; Let me know when I am being prideful, because when I get full of myself, I cannot be full of You. Amen.

*

December 13th

"Humanly speaking it is impossible. But with God everything is possible."

MATTHEW 19:26

Although God isn't a genie, He does have an incredibly deep reserve for each and every one of us. Before we open our mouths, we have to open our hearts.

We also need to realize that everything that happens, good or not so hot, does so in His perfect plan.

Dear God; Let me never limit You, for You have no limits. Amen.

*

December 14th
...Always think carefully before pronouncing judgment. Remember that you do not judge to please people but to please the Lord. He will be with you when you render the verdict in each case that comes your way.

2 CHRONICLES 19:6

My favorite place to people-watch (and people-judge, I admit shame-facedly) is the mall. Why should it matter to me if someone's jeans are too tight or a color I wouldn't wear or their shoes are the trend of the day that doesn't measure up to my standards? It isn't my standard everyone is supposed to measure up to anyway. I'm trying to pass off each judgmental thought that comes my way by asking myself if it really matters in the scheme of things. If the answer is "no", I go on my merry way.

Dear God; I want to use Your criteria to judge everyone and everything. In Jesus' name. Amen.

*

December 15th
Jesus replied, "Every plant not planted by My heavenly Father will be rooted up."

MATTHEW 15:13

How wonderful to think of myself as a plant nurtured by God. Down on His big knees with this tiny seedling in His huge, loving hands, He plants me into the soft ground that He once made Adam out of. Then He waters me and positions His sunshine at just the right angle, all the while talking softly. How could I ever want to be uprooted?

Dear God; You are the Gardener, I am the seed. Let this plant be pleasing to You. Amen.

*

December 16th
You will be accepted if you respond in the right way. But if you refuse to respond correctly, then watch out! Sin is waiting to attack and destroy you, and you must subdue it.

GENESIS 4:7

Subduing sin is easier said than done.

It's hard when I know how God wants me to respond, but my flesh is pulling me in the opposite direction. As with anything else, it is easy to say that we'll say "yes" to God without hesitation, but we never know how we'll react in any given situation.

Dear God; Let my response be such that I subdue my sin. In Jesus' name. Amen.

*

December 17th
I lie awake thinking of You, meditating on You through the night.
PSALM 63:6

When I am oh-so-tired, but I can't sleep (especially when I have re-arranged my schedule to accommodate a nap), I talk to God. I try to make it a real talk, not just a whining session, and I also try not to blame inappropriate behavior on tiredness. That's too easy.

Dear God; When the part of Fibromyalgia that is sleeplessness comes for an unwanted visit, help me to realize that I have the privilege of spending time with You. Amen.

*

December 18th
Spare me so I can smile again before I am gone and exist no more.
PSALM 39:13

We were made in His image, that's why I like smiles so much. They come right from God. He made so many things to provoke smiles in our lives, if we just take a second to find them. It would be a shame not to comply with God.

Dear God; How clever!! Only two muscles does it take to show the world our best feature! Amen.

*

December 19th
I tell you, use your worldly resources to benefit others and make friends. In this way, your generosity store up a reward for you in heaven.

LUKE 16:9

What fun is "success" if we can't share it? The best part of that is to do as much as we can, keeping it between God and us. Not only money or possessions that we were going to get rid of anyway, but time is also a very sharable commodity.

Dear God; My generosity stores up a reward in heaven, but I also get the reward of joy here. Amen.

*

December 20th
For the Lord is your security. He will keep your foot from being caught in a trap.

PROVERBS 3:26

Think of a security system, or a security blanket. Neither of those feelings is comparable to the security He brings.

He knows all, sees all, does all, and loves all. What could bring that calm, safe feeling better than that?

Dear God; For those of us who have Fibromyalgia affecting our legs and feet, this promise means that much more. You are our security, our comfort. Thank You. In Jesus' name. Amen.

*

December 21st
...Give to Caesar what belongs to him. But everything that belongs to God must be given to God.

MATTHEW 12:17

Whenever I get too attached to something, I ask myself if it will get me into Heaven. When I give myself the answer, I go get my Bible or at least say a prayer. If I'm ever in doubt, I figure it out this way: if it's alive, it's God's, if not, it belongs to the world (which is where it will stay).

Dear God; I want to belong to only You, not the world. Let me leave the world alone and be Yours. Amen.

*

December 22nd
And David became more and more powerful because the Lord Almighty was with him.

1 CHRONICLES 11:9

God is always with us. We are God-powered people. If we bought it per gallon, like gasoline, it would be priceless, but it will last a lifetime (and beyond). God-power is a great feeling. Even though we have this supernatural strength, we don't have to wear super-hero costumes to make it work. We just have to "be".

Dear God; You are with each of us. All we have to do is say "yes" to You and Your power. Amen.

*

December 23rd
Your road led through the sea, your pathway through the might waters - a pathway no one knew was there.

PSALM 77:19

We each have a God-appointed path to follow. Sometimes we have no clue where that path is. He does, and He sees it clearly, bright and shiny, all the way to its end. Although He alone knows how it will end, we know where it begins; in a manger in Bethlehem.

Dear God; Let me find that secret pathway so that I can be led away from pain and discouragement right to You. In Jesus' name. Amen.

*

December 24th
And His name will be the hope of all the world.

MATTHEW 12:21

Although God sent His Son, the real gift was hope. Every time a baby is born into the world, hope for the human race is born with it. It all started with Jesus. If we live our lives by using Jesus as our example, we are living the way God wants us to live.

Dear God; Jesus. What a beautiful sound. Shouted (except in vain) or whispered or anywhere in between. You grew in Mary's womb to live in all our hearts. Amen and Amen.

*

December 25th
When they saw the star, they were filled with joy.

MATTHEW 2:10

Even though most of the people saw Mary and Joseph as a young couple about to become parents, everyone who saw their Baby knew that this little boy was somehow very special. The peace, calm, and love of that very first Christmas is in all our hearts; even so many years later.

Dear God; Happy Birthday, Jesus! My heart is so joyful that my heart won't stray from You for a second. Amen.

*

December 26th
For I can do everything through Christ who gives me the strength I need.

PHILIPPIANS 4:13

This was the very first Bible verse I ever memorized. It fits so many situations. It's great for either physical or emotional strength. It's easy to recall in times of turmoil. It's an easy way to refuel when necessary. It's been a real life preserver for me over the years.

Dear God; I can do all that You want me to do through Christ, despite Fibromyalgia. Amen.

*

December 27th

And I will give you the keys to the Kingdom of Heaven. Whatever you lock on earth will be locked in Heaven, and whatever you open on earth will be opened in Heaven.

MATTHEW 16:19

The only possessions we can take to Heaven with us aren't the latest "things" we bought at the mall's big sale. They aren't even what we got for Christmas the day before yesterday.

It is, however, what we got out of Christmas.

Dear God; No Pandora's boxes in Heaven. No strongholds, either. Amen.

*

December 28th

Every word of God proves true. He defends all who come to Him for protection.

PROVERBS 30:5

God cannot lie. It goes against His nature. It would be like an apple tree growing peaches. In this world of scams, isn't it nice to know that every word of His is true? Every word. Every single one. That's a great feeling.

Dear God; You cannot lie. That is the enemy's territory, not Yours. Whenever I come to You, I know the truth will protect me. Thank You. Amen.

*

December 29th

But You, O Lord, are a shield around me, my glory, and the One who lifts my head high.

PSALM 3:3

The ability to hold our heads up high is priceless. We need shields in our lives. It's great to know that we have only one really indestructible shield at our disposal.

All we have to do to accept it is say "yes".

Dear God; Once a person becomes a Christian, it is hard to feel inadequate, have low self-esteem, or throw oneself a "pity-party". Help me to keep my head high as I look up to keep my eyes on You. Amen.

*

December 30th
If you are kind only to your friends, how are you different from anyone else? Even pagans do that.

MATTHEW 5:47

It's easier to be a blessing to those we know well. I mean that it's easier to know their likes and dislikes when it comes to gift giving, card-sending, etc. Our best friends were once strangers. There are countless ways to perform a kindness to those who are not our "friends", whether we do it anonymously or not.

Dear God; Let me show kindness to strangers without distrust of them (because my trust of You is stronger). Amen.

*

December 31st
You crown the year with a bountiful harvest; even the pathways overflow with abundance.

PSALM 65:11

I've always used New Year's Eve day to reflect on my year. An examination of conscience and a long talk with God are part of that reflection. I try not to play "shoulda-woulda-coulda", or turn the day into a "pity-party". Of course, it is also fun to look back at all the happy, crazy times, as well as to look ahead to the New Year.

Dear God; As I reflect on my year, let me count the small, everyday smiles that You have given me among my many blessings. Thank you for a wonderful year behind and one ahead, yet to come. Amen and Amen.

* * *

Printed in the United States
5690